BTEC
Entry 3/Level 1

BUSINESS ADMINISTRATION

ENTRY LEVEL 3/1

Conrad Tetley

Student Book

A PEARSON COMPANY

Published by Pearson Education Limited, a company incorporated in England and Wales, having its registered office at Edinburgh Gate, Harlow, Essex, CM20 2JE. Registered company number: 872828

www.pearsonschoolsandfecolleges.co.uk

Edexcel is a registered trademark of Edexcel Limited

Text © Pearson Education Limited 2010

First published 2010

13 12 11 10
10 9 8 7 6 5 4 3 2 1

British Library Cataloguing in Publication Data
A catalogue record for this book is available from the British Library

ISBN 978 1 846 90921 4

Edited by Liz Cartmell and Janine de Smet
Designed by Pearson Education Limited
Typeset by Tek-Art
Cover design by Pearson Education Limited
Cover photo/illustration © Getty Images/Digital Vision Thomas Barwick
Back cover photos © Shutterstock/Yuri Arcurs and Masterfile/George Remington
Printed in the UK by Scotprint

Disclaimer
This material has been published on behalf of Edexcel and offers high-quality support for the delivery of Edexcel qualifications.

This does not mean that the material is essential to achieve any Edexcel qualification, nor does it mean that it is the only suitable material available to support any Edexcel qualification. Edexcel material will not be used verbatim in setting any Edexcel examination or assessment. Any resource lists produced by Edexcel shall include this and other appropriate resources.

Copies of official specifications for all Edexcel qualifications may be found on the Edexcel website: www.edexcel.com

Contents

About your BTEC E3/L1 Business Administration Student Book   v

About the author

Conrad Tetley has ten years teaching experience working at a large specialist business and enterprise college in Bradford. During that time he has taught a range of academic and vocational courses from BTEC Entry Level to Level 3. Conrad is a Member of the Chartered Institute of Assessors and an accredited Teacher Learning Academy Verifier. He has been involved in developing qualifications at national and regional levels for a number of years and has recently contributed to Edexcel's Level 2 Higher Business, Administration and Finance Diploma textbook.

Credits

The authors and publisher would like to thank the following individuals and organisations for permission to reproduce photographs:

Getty Images/Iconica p. **1**; Shutterstock/Yegorius p. **2**; iStockPhoto/ Chris Schmidt p. **7**; iStockPhoto/Roland Frommknecht p. **8**; iStockPhoto/ Marcus Clackson p. **13**; Shutterstock/Monkey Business Images p. **17**; Shutterstock/Pavol Kmeto p. **20**; Photolibrary/Novastock p. **23**; Alamy Images/fStop p. **24**; Shutterstock/Robert Milek p. **24**; Shutterstock/ Theodore Scott p. **24**; Shutterstock/oksana2010 p. **24**; Shutterstock/ blueking p. **25**; Shutterstock/MAFord p. **25**; Pearson Education Ltd/Devon Olugbenga Shaw p. **27**; Shutterstock/dani3315 p. **28**; Shutterstock/Eray Haciosmanoglu p. **28**; Getty Images/Stockdisc p. **31**; Alamy Images/Edwin Remsberg p. **32**; Pearson Education Ltd/Lord & Leverett p. **38**; Photolibrary/Flirt Collection p. **45**; Alamy Images/ Moodboard p. **44**; Masterfile/George Remington p. **57**; Shutterstock/ Andrey Arkusha p. **58**; Getty Images/Taxi p. **60**; Alamy Images/Michael Pearcy p. **67**; Shutterstock/James Peragine p. **68**; Shutterstock/2happy p. **79**; Shutterstock/Peter Elvidge p. **80**; Shutterstock/Elena Elisseeva p. **91**; Getty Images/Iconica p. **92**; Shutterstock/Yuri Arcurs p. **101**; Shutterstock/Ioana Drutu p. **102**; Masterfile p. **113**; Shutterstock / Marcel Mooij p. **114**; Shutterstock/StockLite p. **116**; Shutterstock/StockLite p. **121**; Shutterstock/3divan p. **129**; Rex Features/Geoffrey Robinson p. **131**; Shutterstock/ifong p. **134**; Shutterstock/macigoven p. **134**; Shutterstock/ Stephen Van Horn p. **134**; Shutterstock/Mickolay Khoroshkov p. **135**; Shutterstock/Haywire Media p.**135**; Shutterstock/Paul Paladin p.**141**

About your BTEC Entry 3/Level 1 Business Administration

Choosing to study for a BTEC Entry 3 or Level 1 Business Administration qualification is a great decision to make for lots of reasons. Many businesses need administrators in order to run smoothly. Behind every successful company there are many administrators, helping to make the organisation focused and effective. As businesses grow they need more skilled administrators who have good communication skills and are well organised. This qualification will help you to develop these skills.

Your BTEC Entry 3/Level 1 Business Administration is a **vocational** or **work-related** qualification. It will give you the chance to gain knowledge, understanding and skills that are important in the subject or area of work you have chosen.

What will you be doing?

This book covers enough units for you to gain any of the following qualifications:

- BTEC Entry 3/Level 1 **Award** in Business Administration

- BTEC Level 1 **Certificate** in Business Administration

In order to complete a BTEC Level 1 **Diploma** in Business Administration you will need to complete another unit from the specification. Our BTEC Entry 3/Level 1 Business Administration Teaching Book and Resource Disk contains Unit 6 in addition to the units covered in this Student Book.

If you are unsure your tutor will let you know what level of qualification you are aiming for.

How to use this book

This book is designed to help you through your BTEC Entry 3/Level 1 Business Administration course. It is divided into 13 units to match the units in the specification. Each unit is broken down into smaller topics.

This book contains many features that will help you get the most from your course.

Introduction

Each chapter starts with a page that gives you a snapshot of what you will be learning from that unit.

MANAGING YOUR HEALTH AT WORK
UNIT 2

When you enter the world of work, you will soon discover that what you do at work and how you complete it can affect your life outside work. Therefore, it is really important to look after yourself so that your body can fight everyday illnesses such as cold, flu, backaches and stress.

Through this unit you will investigate why staying healthy is important and learn how to keep well so that you can stay fit and healthy while working.

In this unit you will:

● Know why it is important to be healthy at work

● Know how to keep healthy at work

What do you think is meant by the term 'work-related illness'?

Activities

You will find activities throughout the book. These will help you understand the information in the unit and give you a chance to try things for yourself.

Activity: Marketing tools

In pairs, create one piece of marketing information, for example, a leaflet, poster or maybe a website to advertise Waite's Weights to both adults and children.

Put some thought into whether the same marketing material will be suitable for both sets of people.

Case studies

Case studies show you how what you are learning about applies in the real world of work.

Case study:
Waite's Weights

Waite's Weights is a gym and health spa business owned and managed by Peter Waite. It is located in Bradford. Throughout the last ten years, Waite's Weights has grown steadily and now employs 25 staff including gym instructors, pool attendants and administrators on a full- or part-time basis.

Before opening his gym, Peter Waite realised that the market for gym and spa memberships was going to grow. The media had repeatedly highlighted that, as a nation, children were taking less exercise. Adults were working longer hours and this was stopping them from taking regular exercise.

So, when the time came to raise funds from banks to open his business, Peter decided to use the examples of school children and working adults as major marketing factors in his business plan.

As time would tell, this was a very good idea which has allowed Waite's Weights to expand. In order to get more customers, Peter Waite advertised a number of gym packages aimed at school children and working adults.

Functional skills

Useful pointers showing you where you can improve your skills in English, Mathematics and ICT.

Functional skills

This activity will help you develop your **English** speaking and listening skills.

Key terms

The words you need to understand are easy to spot, and their meanings are clearly explained.

Key term

Sport
An activity that involves physical exertion and competition.

Remember!

Look out for these boxes. They point out really important information.

! Remember

When receiving instructions, try the technique below to make sure you understand what you're being asked to do.

1. Listen to the instructions.
2. If you are uncertain of anything, ask.
3. Repeat the instructions back to the person who gave them.
4. Ask them to **confirm** your understanding by asking 'Is there anything else?'

Check

You'll find a reminder of key information at the end of each topic.

 ### Check

- It is important to manage your health at work so that you remain fit and able to do your duties.
- Keeping fit will also help with your enjoyment of work.

Assessment page

This page will help you check what you have done so far and give you tips for getting the best mark you can for each task.

Assessment overview ●

This table shows you what assessment criteria you need to meet to pass the unit and on which pages you will find activities and information to help you prepare for your assignments.

Edexcel's assignment tips ●

At the end of each chapter, you'll find hints and tips that will help you get the best mark you can.

Your book is just part of the exciting resources from Edexcel to help you succeed in your BTEC course. Visit www.edexcel.com/BTEC or www.pearsonfe.co.uk/BTEC2010 for more details.

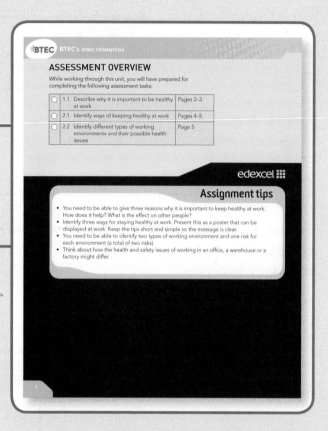

MANAGING YOUR HEALTH AT WORK

When you enter the world of work, you will soon discover that what you do at work and how you complete it can affect your life outside work. Therefore, it is really important to look after yourself so that your body can fight everyday illnesses such as cold, flu, backaches and stress.

Through this unit you will investigate why staying healthy is important and learn how to keep well so that you can stay fit and healthy while working.

In this unit you will:

- Know why it is important to be healthy at work

- Know how to keep healthy at work

What do you think is meant by the term 'work-related illness'?

L01 The importance of being healthy at work

While at work it is important to take your health seriously so that you stay healthy and avoid any problems with illness. This will also help to make sure that the work you produce is free from mistakes which you might make if you felt unwell.

Also, if you are free from illness and managing to keep on top of your work, it normally leads to more enjoyment at work. Enjoying work is an important factor in how well you do your job. If you are successful you may get recognised for this and may be offered promotion or possibly a wage rise. For most people this would increase their levels of self-confidence and self-esteem.

Effects of unemployment

Sometimes people have to face spells of unemployment in their working lives. However, it is often the approach a person takes after they have been made unemployed which shows how successful they will be in the future.

Unemployment not only means someone earns less or no money, it can also be costly in other ways, including affecting their physical and mental health. If people are unemployed for long periods of time, confidence and self-esteem can be affected. This can make someone fearful of applying to organisations for work.

Key term

Promotion
When your employer rewards you by giving you a more important job. It often means earning more money.

Case study:
Waite's Weights

Waite's Weights is a gym and health spa business owned and managed by Peter Waite. It is located in Bradford. Throughout the last ten years, Waite's Weights has grown steadily and now employs 25 staff including gym instructors, pool attendants and administrators on a full- or part-time basis.

Before opening his gym, Peter Waite realised that the market for gym and spa

memberships was going to grow. The media had repeatedly highlighted that, as a nation, children were taking less exercise. Adults were working longer hours and this was stopping them from taking regular exercise.

So, when the time came to raise funds from banks to open his business, Peter decided to use the examples of school children and working adults as major marketing factors in his business plan.

As time would tell, this was a very good idea which has allowed Waite's Weights to expand. In order to get more customers, Peter Waite advertised a number of gym packages aimed at school children and working adults.

Activity: Group discussion

Why do you think Peter Waite thought it was important for school children and working adults to be healthy at school and work?

Which other target groups might Peter Waite want to attract in the future?

Activity: Marketing tools

In pairs, create one piece of marketing information, for example, a leaflet, poster or maybe a website to advertise Waite's Weights to both adults and children.

Put some thought into whether the same marketing material will be suitable for both sets of people.

✓ Check

- It is important to manage your health at work so that you remain fit and able to do your duties.

- Keeping fit will also help with your enjoyment of work.

L02 How to keep healthy at work

Below are some of the most common **health issues** found in the workplace.

Health issue	How it is caused
Backache	Poor posture or unsuitable chair
Aching wrists and fingers	Poor wrist and hand positioning when typing
Weight gain	Eating too much and not exercising enough
Eye strain	Working in poorly lit conditions
Viruses, e.g. cold/sore throat	Sometimes caused by sharing equipment, e.g. telephones
Aching legs	Caused by poor seating position

As an employee of a business you should think about how you can stay healthy for work. After all, you are not much use to an employer if you keep having time off because you are sick. It is therefore important to know a few simple ways in which you can try to keep yourself healthy. Below are a few ideas that may help:

✱ Key terms

Health issue
A potential problem in the workplace that may affect a person's health.

Poor posture
Positioning of the body which could cause long-term damage while working. Always try to adopt the correct posture.

Make sure the temperature of your working environment is comfortable

Avoid poor posture by using a suitable chair

Manage your workload to avoid stressful situations

Make sure you get enough sleep

Ideas for keeping healthy

Avoid arm/wrist strain by using a wrist support

When lifting heavy objects use lifting equipment

Eat a healthy diet in and out of work

Exercise outside work to stay fit

Take regular breaks to avoid wrist/eye strain

When dealing with hazardous materials wear protective clothing

Below are some health factors to consider when working in different environments.

Health factor	Type of environment	Problems caused by health factor at work
Sickness	Hospital	Could pass on virus to patients which could be dangerous
Dizziness	Driving environment	Could cause an accident injuring self and others
Epilepsy	Nightclub	Flashing lights could potentially cause an epileptic seizure
Back strain	Warehouse	Lifting could cause back problems to get worse which may result in a long-term injury
Serious viral throat infection	Call centre/office	Could pass on illness through use of shared equipment, e.g. telephones

Case study:
Waite's Weights services

Waite's Weights offers the following gym and spa services:

- Health spa (including swimming pool, sauna, steam room)
- Beauty services (including nails, facials, etc.)
- Gym (including rowing machines, spinning bikes, weight machines, weights).

Activity: Advertising Waite's Weights

Look at the table on page 4 which explores health issues at work and at the table above which lists five factors that should be considered when working in different environments.

Create one brochure for Waite's Weights which advertises how the business could help people to avoid these problems. Your brochure needs to tie together how the services offered by Waite's Weights can help people to avoid suffering from health issues such as these.

When you have completed your brochure, present your ideas to the rest of your group.

Check

- Make sure you know how to adapt your environment so that you stay healthy at work
- Be aware of how different working environments present a range of potentially different health issues.

ASSESSMENT OVERVIEW

While working through this unit, you will have prepared for completing the following assessment tasks:

◯	1.1	Describe why it is important to be healthy at work	Pages 2–3
◯	2.1	Identify ways of keeping healthy at work	Pages 4–5
◯	2.2	Identify different types of working environments and their possible health issues	Page 5

edexcel

Assignment tips

- You need to be able to give three reasons why it is important to keep healthy at work. How does it help? What is the effect on other people?

- Identify three ways for staying healthy at work. Present this as a poster that can be displayed at work. Keep the tips short and simple so the message is clear.

- You need to be able to identify two types of working environment and one risk for each environment (a total of two risks).

- Think about how the health and safety issues of working in an office, a warehouse or a factory might differ.

WORKING IN BUSINESS & ADMINISTRATION

The term administration covers a very broad area. If on completion of this course you obtain a job or go on to study this aspect of business in more detail, you may specialise in one particular area. Within administration there are many exciting and varied jobs such as working in a marketing department or maybe in IT support. However, all of these jobs will require a core set of skills which you will learn about in this unit.

This unit will give you an introduction to what it's like working in this important area.

In this unit you will:

- Know what activities are routinely undertaken by administrators
- Be able to follow instructions to carry out administrative tasks

Why do you think a big business needs administrators?

The role of an administrator

In business, administration is a range of tasks that need to be completed for the organisation to work effectively. This means that administrators perform an important function, helping managers, sales people, etc. to focus on making the organisation successful.

Case study:
Malek's Motors

Malek's Motors is a car dealership in Bristol, run by Azeem Malek. The business employs two sales people, Carlos and Sharon, and Azeem deals with the business management.

Customers looking for cars make appointments with Malek's Motors to organise test drives. In order to book a test drive, the customer must show their driving licence and proof of identity to one of the sales staff. The business needs to keep a copy of these documents to cover their customers on their insurance.

Malek's Motors is getting more and more customers. Azeem is very pleased – this means more money! However, he, Carlos and Sharon are finding it difficult to keep track of the different test drive bookings, meetings and documents that they have to deal with each day.

Activity: Group discussion

You think Azeem should employ an administrator. As a group, identify the different tasks you think an administrator would do if they worked at Malek's Motors.

How would this help Azeem to make his business more successful?

How do administrators help a business?

A business will have a number of different functional areas. These may include some of the following:

Business function	Purpose
Sales	Selling products or services to customers. The sales department is important because it brings money into the business.
Marketing	The marketing department will advertise the business's products or services. They often work very closely with the sales department.
Finance	The finance department will manage the business's money. It will make sure that the customers pay for the products or services they receive. It will also make sure that the business pays any money it owes.
Production	Not all businesses have a production department. Businesses that make and sell products will probably have one. This department will make the products the business sells.

All the departments in a business will have their own administrative tasks. These may involve keeping copies of financial documents, sending out letters, sending invoices to customers, and many more tasks.

As a business becomes more successful, so the amount of administration each department needs to keep on top of grows. One or more administrators can help the business department to focus on their individual functions by completing the department's administrative tasks.

Key term

Functional areas
Different parts or departments of a business that focus on a limited range of important tasks.

Activity: Group discussion

Working in small groups, choose one business function and identify three different administrative tasks that the function might need help with.

How could this help a business be more effective?

Check

- Administrators help businesses to run smoothly by providing support to business functions.
- Businesses have a range of different functions. They may share an administrator between different functional areas, or each functional area may have its own administrator.

Administrative tasks

Below and opposite are some of the tasks that administrators commonly perform.

Answering the telephone	The administrator is the first point of contact for customers or suppliers. The administrator can direct callers to the people within the organisation that they need to talk to.	Good
Filing and retrieving documents	Organisations need to keep a lot of information. This information may be about customers, suppliers, products, etc. and may need to be accessed at any time. The administrator will use good filing techniques to make it easy to access this information.	Good organisational skills The administrator may also need good IT skills as the filing may be electronic as well as paper-based
Producing documents using IT	Different types of documents need to be produced quickly and effectively. The administrator may also use tools such as mail merge to send the same information to many different people or organisations.	Good IT skills

Activity: How am I doing?

Look at the skills administrators need. How do you think you rate for each skill?

Give yourself a score for each from 1 to 5, with 1 being an area for improvement and 5 being excellent.

Talking to someone – or a group of people – to give them information.

Task	How this helps the organisation	Skills needed
Photocopying and collating documents	A manager may need many copies of the same document to hand out at a presentation, for example. The administrator would save the manager time by photocopying and collating the documents.	Good IT skills
Collecting, sorting and distributing mail	A big organisation will receive a lot of mail each day. The administrator will make sure the mail gets to the right people.	Good organisational skills Good communication skills – it's important to know who everyone is
Receiving visitors	Organisations have a lot of different visitors, from customers to suppliers. The administrator will help organise meetings and will make sure the visitors see the right people.	Good verbal communication skills Professional behaviour

Activity: Routine tasks

Now look at the tasks you identified for an administrator working for Malek's Motors (page 8). Can you identify any other tasks that an administrator would need to perform?

What skills do you think an administrator working for Malek's Motors would need? Working in pairs, use the tables to suggest the skills the administrator would need.

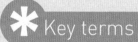

Key terms

Collate
To mix copies of different documents together to give information in a specific order.

Professional behaviour
Acting in a business-like manner. When receiving visitors, answering the phone, etc., you are the public face of your employer. First impressions of an organisation are as important as first impressions of a person.

Check

- Administrators need good IT skills, strong verbal communication skills and have to be well organised.

- Administration involves a range of different tasks.

Understanding and following instructions

As an administrator you need to be able to follow instructions accurately (i.e. without mistakes). This is because you will often be completing a task for someone else – on their behalf – and they may need the task completed in a specific way.

For example, when receiving a visitor for a meeting you might be given specific instructions. These could include:

- Contacting the other meeting attendees so they are aware that the visitor has arrived
- Getting the visitor to sign the visitors' book
- Taking the visitor to the meeting room
- Arranging for a drink for the visitor.

To check that something is right. For example, if you've missed anything, the instructor should be able to tell you what else you need to do.

When receiving instructions, try the technique below to make sure you understand what you're being asked to do.

1. Listen to the instructions.

2. If you are uncertain of anything, ask.

3. Repeat the instructions back to the person who gave them.

4. Ask them to   your understanding by asking 'Is there anything else?'

Activity: Instruction ladder

1. One person should think of some instructions for a skill they use either in the workplace or in a hobby. This shouldn't be anything too complicated, so it may only be part of a task.

2. They explain the steps that need to be completed to a partner who uses the listening technique above to check their understanding.

3. The partner then gives the instructions to the next person, and so on, until everyone in the class has been given the instructions.

Functional skills

This activity will help you develop your English speaking and listening skills.

Case study:
Malek's Motors

Malek's Motors has employed you as an administrator. Azeem is presenting a range of cars to a local business that is looking into leasing a fleet of cars.

This is an important presentation because the deal would earn Malek's Motors a lot of money. Azeem needs to look professional and well organised in order to give the business confidence in him.

Azeem has produced a PowerPoint presentation and a spreadsheet. The presentation contains photos and basic information about the cars. The spreadsheet includes information about how much each type of car would cost the business.

Activity: Paired discussion

Why do you think it would be important for you to follow Azeem's instructions carefully?

What should you do if you are uncertain of what Azeem is asking you to do?

Check

- Always make a note of the important information in any instructions you receive.
- Check you understand the instructions and ask questions if you need to. This will help you do a better job.

Case study:
Malek's Motors

Malek's Motors has a new customer. Azeem's presentation to the business interested in a fleet of cars went very well. They have asked for a   . Azeem has written a letter to the manager of the business, Derek Smith.

He has asked you to type the letter and check it for spelling errors. The letter is on the opposite page. He would like it to be printed and addressed to Derek's business: Smith's Taxis, The Square, Cranbrook Road, Bristol.

Azeem would like a copy of the letter to be filed in case he needs to check the quote at a later date.

Activity: Individual activity

On a piece of paper, produce a   to show the steps you need to go through in order to complete this activity.

By presenting information, you will be demonstrating your speaking skills.

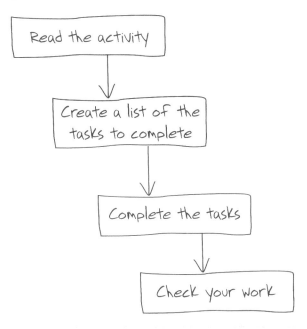

Your flow chart may need more or fewer steps than the example shown here.

Activity: You are the administrator

Follow Azeem Malek's instructions in the case study on the opposite page. Check your work against your flow chart to make sure you complete all the steps you need to.

Dear Derek,

Following on from our meeting last Tuesday, I am pleased to enclose a quote for the lease of eight people carriers from Malek's Motors. These vehicles will be brand new, and as we discussed, we will service them at 12 months or 12,000 miles, whichever is sooner.

The lease of the eight vehicles for a period of 36 months will cost £23,000 per annum. Over the three-year period, this will be £69,000 including VAT at 17.5%.

If you would like any further details, please don't hesitate to get in touch. I look forward to working with you.

Yours sincerely,

Azeem Malik

Now check your work to make sure it's accurate and correct.

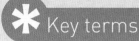

Key terms

Formal quote
This is when a business puts together a set of costs for a customer. For example, if you wanted to buy a computer, you might ask for a quote for a particular model. This would tell you how much you would pay if you decided to buy the computer.

Flow chart
A list of tasks or stages that need to be completed, linked together in a specific order. Some tasks will need to be completed before others can be started. For example, you would need to type the letter in word-processing software before spell checking it.

Functional skills

This activity will help you to practise your ICT skills.

Check

- Work out what you need to do to complete a task.
- Complete the task.
- Check that you have done everything you have been asked to.

ASSESSMENT OVERVIEW

While working through this unit, you will have prepared for completing the following assessment tasks:

◯	1.1	Identify routine administrative tasks	Pages 8–11
◯	2.1	Check understanding of instructions and ask for clarification where necessary	Pages 12–13
◯	2.2	Follow instructions to complete a limited range of administrative tasks accurately	Pages 14–15

Assignment tips

- Ask someone who works in an administrative role to tell you about their day-to-day work.

- From what they tell you, you should be able to identify four routine office tasks.

- When listening to instructions remember to repeat the tasks back to the person.

- Remember, never be afraid to ask if you are not clear what you are being asked to do.

WORKING IN BUSINESS & ADMINISTRATION

When working in business administration it is important to be flexible and comfortable with learning new skills. As an administrator, you may be expected at times to complete several jobs at once. It is therefore very important to be able to adapt to learning new and quicker ways of completing tasks.

While you are working you will also be expected to present yourself and the business you work for in a positive manner. One way of doing this is to complete your work to deadline and to handle sensitive information professionally.

In this unit you will:

- Understand the role of an administrator within an office
- Be able to carry out routine administrative tasks
- Be able to present yourself positively
- Be able to organise your work effectively
- Know the importance of confidentiality of information

What tasks do you think an administrator will do as part of their job?

L01 Understand the role of an administrator

Administrators play a very important role in the smooth running of an organisation. They are responsible for many different tasks which, if not completed successfully, could cause major problems for a business.

Different activities carried out by administrators are shown in the table below.

Producing documents using IT	For example, writing letters to tell customers, suppliers or other organisations about something that is happening that may affect them.	A problem may occur such as a customer receiving an order late. This may affect the customer's business, for example if they will not have products to sell as a result.
Checking, collating and providing information	Businesses receive a lot of information each day. This could include post, and catalogues. An administrator will collect mail and make sure it gets to the right person, file important documents, and obtain information when it is needed.	Important information and notices might not get through to the correct person. This could result in late deliveries, or late payments of invoices, or lost orders. This could cost the business money.
Coordinating arrangements for meetings	A business meeting may involve several people from different organisations. For example, a meeting could be between a sales representative, a marketing executive and a supplier. The meeting could be held at the supplier's office. An administrator would send information to the meeting attendees beforehand, book a meeting room, make sure the meeting was in everyone's calendar and arrange any necessary travel.	If all do not have the correct information in advance of the meeting, including travel details, it might not happen. This can result in the supplier having a poor impression of the business, and possibly taking their trade elsewhere.
Receiving visitors	Companies often have a member of staff working on reception as it presents a professional image to customers or visitors. It also makes sure that people are directed to where they need to go so security is improved.	If a receptionist is rude to a visitor or customer this will give them a bad impression of the company which could result in them going elsewhere. Also, if visitors are not signed in properly, there is no accurate record of who is in the building in the event of a fire.

Task	Why it is carried out	What could happen if task is incorrectly completed
Answering the telephone and making phone calls	Companies use the telephone to communicate with each other as it is quick and effective. Often callers like to talk to someone as it gives them confidence that their request will be carried out. Also, it is seen by some businesses as good customer service to encourage person-to-person communication.	If an employee cannot answer the caller's query, or does not know who to transfer the person to, this will give an unprofessional image of the business and the caller may decide to go elsewhere in the future. Also, if the person who answers the call is not polite, customers may be put off dealing with the business.
Preparing outgoing mail	To make sure that mail is sent to the right place it is important that it is prepared correctly. In preparing mail, the sender must check that the mail is securely packaged, addressed and the correct amount of postal fees paid. Many businesses these days rely on the Internet to sell by mail order only. These businesses will send out a lot of mail, and it is important for their customers that products are delivered effectively. Also, other businesses often rely on the efficient delivery of mail so they can meet the needs of their customers.	If an employee accidentally uses the wrong address or doesn't pay the right postage the customer may not receive their mail. This will annoy customers. If this situation happens often, customers will lose trust in the business and go elsewhere. The business will also develop a reputation for bad customer service.

Activity: Administrator – job description

Imagine you work in the human resources department of a business. You have been asked to write a job description for the new position of sales administrator.

Use the tasks listed in the table to write a description of what you think the job would involve. Then try to identify the skills a sales administrator might need.

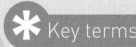
Key terms

Invoice
A document sent to customers requesting payment for the supply of goods or services.

Delegate
Someone attending a meeting. This person may represent another business, and so will want to give a positive impression of their organisation.

Check

- Administrators need to be well organised, especially if they are filing important documents that will be needed at a later date.

- It is important for an administrator to know a lot of different people within the organisation to make sure visitors, telephone calls and mail go to the right people.

Case study:
Sinfield's Supplies

Sinfield's Supplies sells catering supplies to hotels, cafés and restaurants. The business is run by Jack Sinfield and employs four staff. They are his two sons, Ryan and Keith, who look after orders and sending goods, Alfie who is the company accountant and Lucy who takes care of all administration tasks within the business.

Recently, Jack has noticed that the business is receiving more complaints from customers than ever before. Few customers are receiving orders on time. He decides to look into the reasons why.

After a short time it becomes clear to Jack that a number of his staff are either:

- Starting work late in the morning

- Leaving early before the end of the working day or

- Taking longer lunch breaks than they are meant to.

In the light of these problems Jack calls a staff meeting to discuss the matter. At the meeting Jack starts by saying that his team of staff is not meeting the goals of the business.

Activity: Group discussion

What do you think Jack meant by 'goals' of the business?

Why do you think Jack told his staff they were not meeting the goals of the business?

How could Jack solve this problem?

Can you think of any other issues that might be causing Sinfield's Supplies problems?

Team communication

It is important in business to work as a team. By doing so, **business goals** can be achieved more easily. However, it is important to understand how to **prioritise** work in order to set team goals. As with any team (a good example being a premier league football team) all members must work towards achieving the same end result. If this is not the case, the team will not succeed.

It is also important when working as a team to communicate very clearly. If this does not happen other team members may not understand instructions and tasks may be carried out incorrectly. Clear communication also covers the use of written, **graphical** and electronic communication methods – again there could be problems if communication is confusing.

Team support

When working as a team member it is very important that you support one another. As with any successful sports team, each member must play their part. In the case of working as an administrator this may involve listening to others to try to resolve a problem or helping another person if they are getting behind with their work.

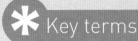
Key terms

Business goal
A business goal is what the business is aiming to do – this might be as simple as make a profit.

Prioritise
Decide on the order for dealing with a number of tasks according to their relative importance.

Graphical communication
The use of visual images such as diagrams, illustrations or designs to convey meaning.

Activity: What does Jack have to do?

Read the Sinfield's Supplies case study to the left again.

Before Jack can take any action he must prioritise which issues are causing him the most problems.

Individually, you need to prioritise Jack's three top issues that he must deal with first. Give reasons for your choices.

Check

- To achieve team goals each group member must be clear what his or her role is and how it helps the team to achieve its overall goal.

- To be an effective team member you must listen and help others.

Carry out routine administrative tasks

From the case study on page 20 it is clear that some of Jack's staff are not carrying out routine tasks as they should be. It is important that, when you work as an administrator, you are able to carry out routine tasks effectively so mistakes do not happen.

Activity: What routine tasks do administrators carry out?

On a plain piece of paper, draw and complete the mind map below showing as many routine administration tasks as you can think of. You might also want to include the skills needed to complete the work correctly.

One example has been completed and a second has been started. Try to add at least eight tasks and as many skills needed as you can think of.

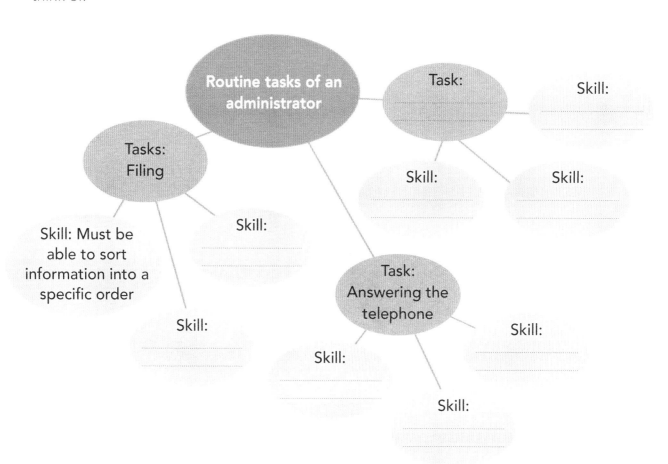

Case study:
Sinfield's Supplies

You have been employed as a general administrator at Sinfield's Supplies. You are expected to provide support where needed. The nature of the job makes it very interesting as you will be able to see how all parts of the business work.

However, as with most jobs, this post does have a number of routine tasks that have to be completed.

Activity: List the tasks

Make a list of the routine administrator tasks you think you will have to carry out.

Why is successful completion of these tasks important to the business?

Which tasks could be completed using ICT?

Following instructions

Administrators need to make sure they follow instructions accurately in order to do their jobs. (For some guidance on following instructions, see *Unit 5 Understanding and following instructions*, page 12.)

Activity: Telephone conversation

In pairs, role play a telephone conversation. One person plays the role of a customer service adviser while the other takes on the role of a customer.

Before you have the conversation the 'customer' needs to write down what they are going to talk about. During the conversation the 'customer service adviser' should write down what they think the customer wants.

At the end of the conversation, compare notes and then swap roles.

! Remember

When receiving instructions, try the technique below to make sure you understand what you are being asked to do.

1. Listen to the instructions.

2. If you are unsure of anything, ask.

3. Repeat the instructions back to the person who gave them.

4. Ask them to confirm you have understood correctly by asking 'Is there anything else?'

Check

- Routine administration tasks are the ones that are completed daily or often.

- Following instructions involves listening carefully and asking questions if you are not sure.

L02 Using office equipment and office etiquette

Office equipment

When working in administration you will need to use many different types of office equipment. Some of these are shown in the table below. It is important that you read the manufacturer's instructions before starting to use them. This is very important for three reasons:

- So you do not damage the equipment

- So you do not injure yourself

- So your work is of a high quality.

Piece of office equipment	What is it used for?
Franking machine	Franking machines are used to automatically stamp letters. Companies use them as it would be too time-consuming to put individual stamps on the hundreds of letters they normally send out every day. Franking machines also have the advantage that the business does not have to go out to buy stamps. Instead it pays the postal company direct.
Printer	
Shredder	
Telephone	

Piece of office equipment	What is it used for?
Fax machine	
Photocopier	

Office etiquette

It is really important to think of others when you are working in an office environment. You will soon become unpopular if you can't be bothered to complete tasks and other people have to do them. However, it is not difficult to keep colleagues happy – it is simply a matter of good manners.

So what can be done to make sure that you play your part and the office you work in runs smoothly? Below are some ideas:

- Make sure that you keep equipment clean and hygienic
- Make sure that you refill printers and photocopiers when you have used them and paper levels are low
- Report any problems to your supervisor – this avoids slowing down the workflow and makes sure others do not get into trouble for damaging machinery
- Keep waste to a minimum by spell checking, reusing scrap paper for notes and double-sided copying
- Separate different types of waste so that it can be recycled
- Be helpful to others who you work with.

Activity: Office etiquette

Carry out research into office etiquette. Prepare a poster that could be pinned up in an office reminding people how to behave professionally.

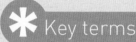
Key terms

Colleague
Someone from the same organisation as you. They could be more junior than you, someone at the same level as you (sometimes called a 'peer'), or someone at a more senior level than you.

Etiquette
Good manners and thinking about other people. It is good etiquette to refill the photocopier because it would be irritating to have to fill it with paper before you wanted to use it each time.

Check

- Instructions for using office equipment are there to protect the user from harm, save the company money and make sure that machinery is used properly.

- Office etiquette is important as you will be expected to behave in a professional manner when working as an administrator.

Health and safety and positive presentation

Health and safety

All employers have a **legal duty** to make sure that employees work in an environment that is safe and free from **risks**. The Act of Parliament which covers this is called the Health and Safety at Work Act.

If a business does not work within the Health and Safety at Work Act, then it can be taken to court and sued if it is found to be at fault. Most businesses take health and safety very seriously and employ staff whose job it is to check health and safety in the workplace.

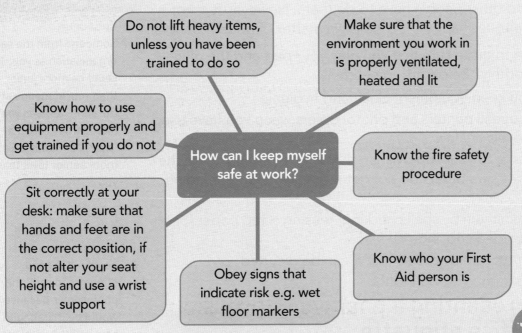

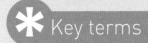 **Key terms**

Legal duty
Something a business has got to do. If a business does not do their legal duty, they could be acting illegally.

Risk
A risk is the chance that something might happen. For example, if wires are trailing across a corridor there is a risk someone could trip over them.

Acronym
Shortening a long name by using the initial letters of each word. For example, the BBC is an acronym for the British Broadcasting Corporation.

Activity: What do the following mean?

Individually, research the following **acronyms** and create a poster which tells other group members what they mean:

- COSHH
- PPE
- RIDDOR
- HSE.
- PUWER

Functional skills

If you use the Internet to research for this activity, you will be practising your **ICT** skills.

Present yourself positively

When working in administration it is important to present yourself in a positive manner so that your colleagues know that you are working towards the same goal as them.

There are many ways in which you can present yourself positively including:

- Dressing professionally for work
- Arriving at work and appointments/meetings on time
- Being constructive towards colleagues and not criticising
- Asking questions so you do not make mistakes
- Making sure you do what you have said you are going to do.

Activity: Role play – dealing with a negative worker

For this role play you will need to work in pairs:

- One person needs to be an employee who is very negative towards their work
- The other person plays the role of the employee's manager in an interview situation. During the role play the manager needs to pay close attention to the manner of the employee and to find out why he or she is negative towards work and discuss possible solutions.

As a starting point, both people need to work together and make a list of reasons why the person is negative towards work. They then need to make another list of possible solutions.

The role play may be scripted or non-scripted.

Activity: Presenting a positive impression

As a group make a list of the top ten tips for making a good impression on others. After you have made your list, discuss it to make sure you have put the tips in the correct order. You may need to change the order of your initial list.

✓ Check

- It is important to follow health and safety legislation so that you do not injure yourself or harm others through your actions.

- When working in business, employers like to see employees presenting themselves in a positive manner.

L05 Organise your work effectively and understand confidentiality

Effective organisation

When working in administration it is very important to organise your work and manage your time effectively, otherwise jobs may get forgotten or not completed.

The good news is that modern technology has made this task very easy and is quite affordable. Devices such as Personal Digital Assistants (PDAs) and mobile phones have changed the way workers organise their workload.

Activity: Comparing PDAs and Smartphones

For this task you need to research at least ten PDAs including Smartphones. You are to compare the features of the devices and then work out which ones would be most suitable for the people below:

- A sales representative
- A middle manager in a bank
- A managing director of a large steel production company.

Prioritising tasks through discussion

Often in business you will be in a situation where two important jobs need to be completed at the same time. However, you only have one set of hands!

In this situation you will need to negotiate with your supervisor which job you are going to complete first. In doing this, you will need to give good reasons why you have chosen to prioritise one job over another.

Activity: Making a 'to do' list

Working individually, think about your next week at your centre and at home. Make a list of all the things you have to do. Then put your list in order of priority. It is often surprising how many things you can fit into one week.

The importance of confidentiality of information

When working for a company it is important that information is kept **confidential**. Reasons for this include:

- Personal details cannot be made available to the public
- Company documents will not get into the wrong hands
- To make sure that the business is working within the Data Protection Act. If a company is found not to be **complying** with the law it can face legal action which usually results in large fines.

Key terms

Confidential
Information that should not be shared, such as salary details, company strategies, customer contact details, etc.

Comply
To act by the guidelines or rules set out in a law, such as the Data Protection Act. It is a business's legal duty to comply with these laws.

! Remember

When storing and using information:

- Never leave confidential information unattended – lock away paper copies and lock your screen when you leave your computer
- Make sure that if you are using a computer with confidential information that your screen is positioned in such a way to stop other people looking at it
- When giving someone else information, be careful – make sure that you know who you are talking to and the amount of information you can tell them
- Set passwords on sensitive files to help keep them secure
- Come up with a list of questions to ask the person that you are shadowing.

◎ Activity: How long should information be stored on file?

For this task, you need to research the different types of information that might be stored on file by businesses. Think about the kind of details you have had to give when buying something over the Internet.

When you have researched this, find out for how long that information can be legally stored – this is called a 'retention period'.

Present your work to your group.

✔ Check

- It is important to organise your work so that tasks get completed on time. Employees will then know they can rely on you and you will soon become a trusted member of staff.

- It is important to know when to share information and when not to. Letting information get into the wrong hands could be costly to you and your business.

ASSESSMENT OVERVIEW

While working through this unit, you will have prepared for completing the following assessment tasks:

○	1.1	Describe different activities carried out by administrators	Pages 18–19
○	1.2	State how the work of an administrator helps a team achieve its goals	Pages 20–21
○	2.1	Follow instructions to complete routine administrative tasks	Pages 22–23
○	2.2	Use key equipment according to organisational procedures	Pages 24–25
○	3.1	Dress appropriately	Page 27
○	3.2	Adopt a positive manner in dealings with colleagues and/or customers	Page 27
○	4.1	Use simple tools to organise your time	Page 28
○	4.2	Prioritise tasks in discussion with your supervisor or manager	Page 28
○	5.1	State the reasons why it is important to keep some information confidential	Page 29
○	5.2	Give examples of information that should be kept confidential	Page 29

edexcel

Assignment tips

- You need to describe four activities carried out by administrators.

- You also need to state two ways in which administrators help achieve team goals.

- Your tutor will need to observe you completing three administrative tasks. They will also need to observe you using at least two types of key equipment.

- You will need to give three reasons why it is important to keep some information confidential. You will also need to give examples of three different types of confidential information. Try to think about the kind of information that might be stored in different systems, and what this might mean for confidentiality.

- You may be able to combine two assessment tasks in one activity if you pick your tasks carefully.

COMMUNICATING ELECTRONICALLY

All administrators need to be able to communicate effectively – both face to face and electronically. As an administrator you will be expected to deal with problems and queries effectively by yourself.

In today's business world much of the work you deal with will be sent to you electronically, as emails and text messages, etc. You will be expected to deal with these in a similar way.

In this unit you will learn about different electronic communication methods and the most suitable methods to use in certain situations.

In this unit you will:

- Be able to communicate electronically
- Be able to use the Internet securely

When do you think it would be appropriate to use text messages to communicate in business? When might it not be appropriate?

L01 Effective communication

Case study:
Mulkern's Foods

Mulkern's Foods is an organic food production and farming company based in Shrewsbury. The business is owned by Jack Mulkern and employs three staff – Simon, Geoff and Bridget. Simon and Geoff are involved with the production and packaging of the food. Bridget is in charge of dealing with all the administration. Jack is responsible for overall management of the business.

Mulkern's Foods mainly sells its goods direct to specialist shops and upmarket pubs and restaurants. However, the business also runs a small shop from its factory. All the staff help to run this shop, taking turns alongside their main roles.

Even though there has been a recession, and customers have been spending less, the shop has been very successful. However, Jack has noticed that while turnover – money coming into the shop – has increased by 50 per cent over the last two years, his profit has only increased by 11 per cent. This is worrying him.

He has asked all staff to check their work processes to find out where they might be spending more money than they need to. After a month, Jack realises that much of this spending is linked to sending correspondence, including letters and invoices, to customers.

Business communication methods

In business you will be expected to communicate with people who work at different levels in the organisation. This may range from an office junior to a director. It is therefore important to know which electronic communication methods are suitable for employees at different levels within the business.

Opposite is a table which shows the suitability of the four main methods you will be investigating.

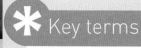**Key terms**

Turnover
Money coming into a business from customers. For example, if a customer buys a pie from Mulkern's shop for £2, this money counts towards the business's turnover.

Profit
Money left over when all costs have been taken out of the turnover. In order to make the pie, Mulkern's Foods needs to spend a total of £1.50 on ingredients, making the pie and cooking the pie. The difference between what Mulkern's Foods spends to make the pie, and the amount the customer pays for the pie, is its profit.

Correspondence
A broad term for any form of written communication. This could include letters, emails, faxes, text messages, etc.

Type of electronic communication method	Where is it appropriate to use it?
Email	Email is probably the communication method used most often in business today. Email has many benefits over 'snail' mail (posted mail) because it is cheap, quick, and different types of documents can be attached.
	Email is appropriate for most office communications. However, some legal communications still have to be written in the traditional way.
Fax	Until email became popular, faxing was a favoured method of communication. This is because you can send an exact copy of a document. Faxing is a quick method of communication unless the telephone line is busy.
	Faxing is appropriate in situations where a person needs to see exactly what another person has sent. It is useful for sending documents such as plans, contracts or orders.
SMS (short message service) text messaging	Texting is now used in business quite often by employees. However, SMS messages cannot contain as much information as emails. They are useful if a person is based in the 'field', i.e. not working in an office, as they can be quickly and cheaply contacted.
	Useful for non-sensitive information or colleague-to-colleague communication.
Internet	The Internet is a very popular method of communication. Companies often use the Internet for marketing and advertising purposes. However, most sites will have a 'Contact' page where you can write to the business if you need to.

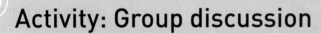

Activity: Group discussion

From the case study it would seem that Mulkern's Foods is quite a traditional company which does not use modern communication technology as well as it could.

1. Identify the different types of communication technology Mulkern's Foods could use to reduce its costs.

2. Why do you think Mulkern's Foods has not used modern technology?

3. Do you think SMS text messaging would be an a suitable method to help reduce Mulkern's Foods' costs?

Check

- The four methods of electronic communication you will need to investigate include emails, faxes, text messages and the Internet.

- It is important that you choose the correct communication method for the type of message you are trying to send.

L01 Communicating with different people

Working as an administrator in the business, you will need to communicate effectively with a range of different people. These may be people within the same business as you (sometimes called 'internal customers') or someone from outside the business (an 'external customer').

The word '**customer**' is very important in both these cases. This is because you should always remember that you are providing a service to these people.

Internal customers

Internal customers are people from the same business as you, i.e. your **colleagues**. They may work in the same department, a different part of the business, or could even be your boss.

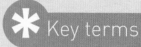

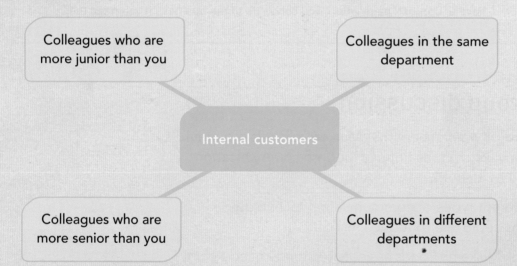

Colleagues who are more junior than you

Colleagues in the same department

Internal customers

Colleagues who are more senior than you

Colleagues in different departments

For example, in the case of Mulkern's Foods (see page 32), Jack might be meeting with an important client to discuss a large order. This would be very important for the business as it could bring in a lot of money. For the meeting, Jack might need the sales history of the client. He would ask Bridget, the administrator, to find the information he needs before the meeting.

It is important that Bridget gets the information to Jack by the time he has asked for it as it could affect the business.

External customers

An external customer is someone from a different organisation from the one you work for. This could be someone buying something from your business, or it could be a supplier. An external customer may be a private individual (a member of the public, not representing anyone else) or representing another business.

When dealing with external customers you must keep the following in mind:

- You are representing your business so make sure you give a good impression

- Everyone is different – some people may not know your business as well as you, or may not be communicating in their first language, so be patient and understanding

- If you can't answer a question, ask someone who can.

Activity: Internal or external?

Read the case study on page 32 again. In pairs, discuss whether the following are examples of internal customers or external customers.

1. Jack asks Simon to pack a selection of Mulkern's Foods' samples for a meeting he will have with a potential customer.

2. Bridget receives a telephone call from a customer who needs to know what time the shop closes.

3. Jacinta is a local cake baker and is meeting Jack to see whether he would be interested in selling her cakes in the shop.

Check

- An internal customer is someone from the same organisation as you.

- An external customer is someone from a different organisation, or a private individual.

L01 Email

Email is electronic mail and in many cases it has taken the place of letters in business communication. Email is fast and – most importantly – cheap, meaning that businesses can cut down on the amount of money it costs to send information to customers and suppliers.

Email basics

You can do a lot of things with email. Some of the basics are explained in the table below.

Term	What this means
cc	This stands for 'carbon copy', which refers to the old way in which businesses made copies of important documents. You cc someone into an email if they need to be aware of the email, but not necessarily do anything about it.
bcc	This stands for 'blind carbon copy'. The person who receives the email will not know that someone has been copied (cc'd) into the communication.
Attachment	Email is often used to send electronic documents. This could include a word-processed file, a digital photograph, a digital video, or even a computer program. You need to be careful when opening attachments as they could contain a nasty surprise, such as a computer virus. Only open attachments from people you know and trust.
Forward	You may have received a question by email that you cannot answer. You can send the email to someone else who would be able to answer the question. This is known as forwarding an email. It is usually polite to add an explanation to the message you are forwarding so the recipient knows what to do with it.

Email etiquette

When using email, it is important to use an appropriate tone. This means that you need to check your work for the following points before sending an email.

- Is your message clear? Will the recipient easily understand the information you are trying to get across? If not, how could you explain it more clearly?

- Is your language appropriate? Try not to be too familiar, but at the same time not too abrupt.

- Are you being polite? Remember to thank someone for their email, or add 'please' to anything you are asking your recipient to do. You will be amazed by how much it helps!

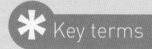
Key terms

Email etiquette
Good practice guidelines. These are things to consider when sending emails, and can help avoid embarrassing cases of misunderstanding.

Tone
The way in which one person speaks to another person.

Recipient
Someone who receives something. In this case, someone who receives an email.

Activity: A catalogue of errors

Geoff from Mulkern's Foods emailed a supplier with a question about a product that he was thinking about ordering for the business. However, when he got the email below in reply, he decided to take his business to another organisation.

```
From: Jackie Shields
To: Geoff Banks
50.
Thanks,
Jackie
```

```
From: Steve Bachmann
To: Jackie Shields
Hey Jackie, how's your head this morning? Ha! That was some night out!
Can you reply to this customer? He obviously hasn't read the catalogue.
S
```

```
From: Geoff Banks
To: Steve Bachmann
Dear Steve,
I am considering ordering several packs of silver foil trays
(catalogue no. 145). Please could you tell me the number of trays
in each pack?
Yours sincerely,
Geoff
```

What is wrong with the email…? What would you suggest Jackie and Steve should do differently?

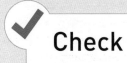

Check

- Always think about your recipient when sending an email. What tone of language is appropriate? What do they need to know?

- Always think twice before opening an attachment – it could cause your computer some harm. Do you know the sender? Are you expecting someone to send you an attachment?

L01 More on emails and faxes

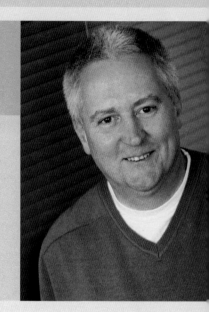

Case study:
Mulkern's Foods

After much discussion and research, Jack Mulkern has decided to spend a lot of money on communication technology and training for his business. However, Jack and his staff know very little about modern communication technology and even less about the correct way to use it.

Jack decides that he needs to call in outside help. He has heard of a company called 'Super Communication Solutions' which provides training on how to use communication technology.

Activity: Presentation

As an employee for Super Communication Solutions, you are going to give a presentation to explain what the following mean – and how to carry out each task – when emailing:

- How to send, forward and reply to an email
- Sending and receiving attachments
- Using cc and bcc
- The type of language that should be used
- What you should do if you receive an email from an unknown user
- Risks of downloading files and software
- Risks of sharing information such as chain emails and personal details.

Prepare and send a fax

Until recently a very common method of communication in business was the use of facsimile, or fax for short. Faxes are useful because the recipient receives an exact copy of what a person is sending.

Even though email can do a similar task, businesses still use faxes as they are the easiest way of quickly sending documents with signatures between people. For example, this might be used for contracts.

When you send a fax, it goes directly to the recipient's fax machine. If you are sending a fax to someone in a large business, the fax machine is unlikely to be at their desk. In order to avoid confusion, you need to include the following information on a cover sheet:

- To: where you print the recipient's name

- From: where you print your name, and the name of your business

- Date: the date on which you are sending the fax

- Pages: the total number of pages faxed, including the cover sheet.

Fax machines

As with most types of electronic equipment, fax machines come in various types, ranging from very simple ones to complex multi-function machines. It is no use having a fax machine if you do not know how to operate it efficiently.

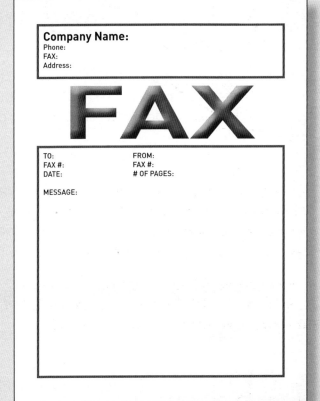

Activity: Create a fax cover sheet for your own business

For this individual activity you need to create a fax header sheet for a business of your choice. You must make sure that all the correct information is contained on the fax cover sheet, including a logo for your business.

 Functional skills

If you use word-processing software to create a fax cover sheet, you may be showing you can use a number of ICT skills.

✔ Check

- Faxes can be used to send a copy of something for which you don't have an exact electronic copy. For example, a signed contract, or an order form sent to you by another business.

- When sending a fax, you need to make sure you include a summary of the number of pages, the sender, the recipient and the date on a cover sheet.

L01 Text messaging

As mobile phones become more advanced, the opportunities for sending different types of messages from your mobile increase. The latest phones allow you to do everything that you can do on a laptop only on a smaller scale.

You can now send emails, **Multimedia Message Service (MMS)** messages and **Instant Messaging (IM)** messages from your phone. However, one basic requirement still exists – the need to make sure what you are sending makes sense and can be understood.

Activity: Encoding a message

For this activity you will work on your own initially and then as part of a group.

1. Think up a complex sentence which relates to business administration and write out the sentence using Standard English (i.e. full words).

2. Convert the message as best you can into text message language. If you are struggling for an abbreviation use the Internet for research – there are plenty of text message dictionaries online.

3. Stand up in front of your group and read out your text message. See how many group members can decode the message correctly.

Multimedia Message Service (MMS)
Allows you to send and receive not only text but also sound, images and video.

Instant Messaging (IM)
An instant text messaging service that happens in 'real time'.

Abbreviate
To make a word shorter, either by taking out letters (e.g. 'tomorrow' becomes 'tmro') or by cutting the word short (e.g. 'Saturday' becomes 'Sat').

Short Message Service (SMS)
Allows you to send or receive text messages only up to 160 characters in length.

SMS text messaging

Short Message Service (SMS) text messaging has become very popular over the last 20 years. This is because it has become more affordable and easy to do. Nearly all mobile phones have a text message facility.

However, in business, texting has its limitations:

- Only a small amount of information can be sent in a text message

- 'Text' language is often not appropriate in a professional situation.

Communications need to be clear and accurate. Uncertainty about the meaning of a message can be very costly to business.

Activity: When to text

Draw and complete the mind map by stating when text messaging is appropriate in business and when it is not, and why.

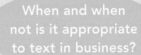

When and when not is it appropriate to text in business?

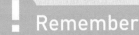

! Remember

- It may be acceptable to use a text message to communicate with a colleague who is out of the office...

- but you need to make sure your message is clear and accurate...

- and fits into 160 or fewer characters.

Activity: Appropriate?

Why would this style of text message not be appropriate for business?

In pairs, make a list of reasons and present what you have found to your group.

Hi Mr Brwn Soz, will be a bit l8 4 meeting. Stk in traffic. Will be thr as soon as! ☹

✓ Check

- Before you send a text message for business purposes, ask yourself if this is the most appropriate way to communicate.

- It is important that any business communication you send from your mobile phone is clear and accurate.

L02 Using the Internet securely

The Internet is a great source of information. With a few clicks of the mouse it is possible to find answers to a huge number of questions. Search engines like Google, Ask or Bing can help you find any information you want.

However, it is important that you use the Internet securely (safely). There are many reasons for this including the security of personal data and avoiding the potential for cybercrime to happen.

To increase Internet safety and security, Internet service providers have developed very advanced systems and software to reduce the risk of problems. However, very often the most basic security measures can have the most effect. For example, always use passwords that are difficult to work out. It is recommended that passwords should be no less than eight characters in length (ideally 12) and contain letters, numbers and characters.

Key term

Cybercrime
A type of crime that uses computers. This can include identity theft, stealing from online bank accounts, stealing information, etc. You have to be very careful with information you give away online to avoid cybercrime.

! Remember

- Information on the Internet is more reliable from some sources than others. Services like Wikipedia can be edited by anyone (but is checked by Wikipedia staff), so might not be 100 per cent accurate. The BBC website is edited and checked on a regular basis.

- Secure websites start their address with https:// (the 's' means 'secure'), and your web browser will show a padlock icon. This means that it is safe to enter personal details. If the website does not display a padlock icon, think carefully before you give any personal information.

◎ Activity: How can I keep my information secure and free from viruses?

In pairs, make an Internet security poster. Discuss the bullet points below in your poster. Explain how they can improve or reduce levels of Internet security.

- Need to keep passwords secure
- Viruses and virus protection
- Firewalls
- Security updates

- Dangers of file sharing
- Letting other people know your personal details
- Giving unauthorised people access to data.

When you have completed your poster, pass it to another group for them to mark out of ten.

When marking another group's work you must provide supportive comments on what is good about their poster and what could be done to improve it.

Using the Internet effectively

As well as using the Internet securely it is important to know how it works. For example, do you know how a search engine works? Do you know how to save results so they can be found and used again in the future?

In simple terms, the Internet is a huge database of information arranged into websites. When you type in what you are looking for in a search engine, all you are doing is instructing the computer to search and find websites that contain the words you have typed in.

Sometimes you may find the search engine will return strange results. Remember a computer is only a machine and the Internet is only a piece of software – they cannot think for themselves. Change your search terms, and see if you can get a better result.

Activity: A day in the life of an administrator

Bridget from Mulkern's Foods is on holiday and has left you a list of things to do. You need to choose the most appropriate electronic communication method to use for each one. Give reasons for your answer.

- Send a completed order form to a supplier for four packs of foil trays.

- Remind Geoff while he is out of the office that he needs to phone The Old Boot in Whittington.

- Find a list of pubs within 50 miles of Shrewsbury for Jack to target with a marketing campaign.

Check

- When finding information on the Internet, make sure you can trust the source. If you are not sure of something, check it with another website.

- Always check whether a web page is secure before entering personal details.

ASSESSMENT OVERVIEW

While working through this unit, you will have prepared for completing the following assessment tasks:

○	1.1 Send, receive and forward emails	Pages 36–37
○	1.2 Prepare and send a fax	Pages 38–39
○	1.3 Prepare and send a clear and accurate text message	Pages 40–41
○	2.1 Log on to the Internet	Pages 42–43
○	2.2 Access an appropriate website showing awareness of security	Pages 42–43

Assignment tips

- You need to think about how you will produce your assessment work for this unit. You can use saved files and printouts. However, your tutor will need to witness you preparing and sending a clear and accurate text message.

- You need to be aware of – and be able to talk through – the security issues around accessing websites. You may need to record conversations with your tutor for this. You could also add notes to screenshots to show your awareness of security issues when using the Internet.

MAKING & RECEIVING CALLS

When working as an administrator, one of the most common tasks you will carry out will be to make and receive telephone calls. It is therefore very important that you learn how to use telephones in line with company rules. A key skill you will need to learn is how to present a positive image to anyone who contacts the company you work for.

In this unit you will:

- Be able to make telephone calls correctly

- Be able to receive telephone calls correctly

- Know why it is important to an organisation that calls are handled appropriately

What do you think are the most important skills for using the telephone effectively?

L01 Making calls

📁 Case study:
Smith's Motorcycles

Andrew Smith decided to open his own motorcycle sales and repairs shop. The business expanded and within three years of opening it employed 20 people. Five worked on the sale and repair of motorcycles and the remaining 15 dealt with customer orders over the telephone and online, as well as carrying out day-to-day administration duties.

However, Andrew's business started losing sales. It was noticeable that there were fewer telephone enquiries than the year before and this worried Andrew.

Karen, the administration manager, had a meeting with Andrew to discuss the situation. She suggested that staff were not dealing appropriately with customers over the telephone.

Identify the purpose of a call

It is important to think carefully about a call before you make it. By understanding clearly the purpose of your call, you can plan what you are going to say to the other person and how you are going to say it. It is important to choose the right words and tone for the situation.

Check the name and number of the person to be called

Have you ever received a telephone call from a person who has got some of your personal details (i.e. name, address, etc.) wrong? If you have an unusual name, this can happen regularly.

While this can be annoying on a personal level, in a business situation it can be costly. After all, if a person is calling from a business that you deal with regularly and cannot get your details correct, what sort of image does that present? Businesses must act professionally at all times if they are to keep a good reputation. This includes knowing the correct name and number of the person being telephoned.

Communicating clearly and accurately

It is important to communicate basic information clearly and in a way that the listener can understand. The checklist below gives some ideas to help you make sure your call is clear and well structured:

- Write down what you are going to say and check it carefully

- Re-write it in a logical sequence (so it is easy to follow what you are saying)

- Write down questions that you want to ask

- Think about how you will answer any questions

- Think about the language and tone of voice you are going to use

- Think about how familiar you are with the person you are calling. This will affect the style of your telephone call.

Remember to summarise the key points at the end of the call so that you are both clear what has been said or agreed.

Activity: Group discussion

Think of a time when you have received poor service over the telephone.

Using this experience, create a telephone script that the administrators at Smith's could use to make sure that customers get the same level of service every time. Think about the following:

- Why is it important for administrators to identify the purpose of a call?

- Why it is important to speak to customers correctly?

- Why are administrators often known as the 'face of the company'?

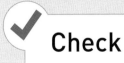

Check

- Clear communication is important when making a telephone call. To avoid any embarrassing problems, plan what you are going to say before you pick up the telephone.

- Make sure that you have the correct number for the person you are calling as this will save time.

L02 Receiving calls

Answering a call promptly and politely observing any organisational procedures

Most organisations will have certain expectations of staff when their job involves answering telephone calls from customers. Many businesses have strict policies that must be followed when staff answer the telephone. For example the phone should be answered in three rings.

If you ever get the chance to visit a call centre, ask one of the call centre telephonists if you can look at their telephone script. A telephone script tells the operator exactly what he or she has to say and the questions to ask a customer.

Policy
A principle or course of action adopted by an organisation or individual.

Activity: Sitting next to Nelly

Ask if your tutor can arrange for you to visit a company where you can spend a short period of time in the office sitting next to a member of staff who is answering telephone calls.

Listen to the language the person uses along with the different ways in which he or she uses the tone of their voice when dealing with different callers. (In the past, it used to be called learning by 'Sitting next to Nelly' if you learned by sitting next to another person!)

Functional skills

When listening to the way someone uses language, you will find you can improve your English learning.

Identifying a caller, where they are calling from and the purpose of their call

It is important to identify correctly where a caller is calling from and the purpose of their call so that you have some idea of what they are calling about. Also, if you are transferring a person to another member of staff, you will need to pass this information on. Identifying callers is all part of presenting a professional image of the business.

The diagram opposite gives you some good pointers when dealing with calls.

1. Ask politely who is calling

2. Find out if the person wishes to speak to you or be transferred to someone else

3. If the person wishes to speak to you – listen carefully and use clear, accurate language

4. Take notes so you do not forget why the person has called. Note their phone number as you may need to phone them back later

5. Always end a phone call by asking if you can help the caller further

Case study:

Smith's Motorcycles

During his meeting with Karen, Andrew discovered that a number of his staff were not taking notes when customers were ringing the business. Karen felt sales were being affected because staff did not always call customers back if they could not answer their questions straightaway. This alarmed Andrew and so he decided to do something about it.

Activity: Providing an efficient service

1. Why might staff not take notes when customers called the business?

2. Suggest how Andrew could improve this situation.

3. How might customers feel about the business if, after being promised, they were not rung back?

Check

- It is important to identify the purpose of a call so that you know how to deal with the caller.

- Answer telephone calls quickly and politely so that you don't keep a customer waiting.

LO2 Confidentiality and security

Organisational procedures

When dealing with telephone calls, it is important that you do not discuss certain things with callers. For example, you are not allowed to discuss another person's personal details without their permission. If you do, you will be breaking the Data Protection Act. This is a complex law and it is designed to protect the use of an individual's information.

If this law is broken you can be held personally liable for prosecution, meaning you could be taken to court and fined.

The key points of the Data Protection Act are outlined below.

Data should not be transferred to other countries without adequate protection

Data should be obtained and processed fairly and lawfully – meaning that the owner normally needs to consent to the information being used

Data should be accurate and up to date

Key points of the Data Protection Act

Data should only be processed for limited purposes

Data, including personal data, should be kept for no longer than necessary

Data must be stored securely

Data which is kept should be adequate and relevant but not excessive

Activity: Data Protection booklet

Individually, prepare a booklet outlining the key points of the Data Protection Act. Use any websites recommended by your tutor to help with your research.

When you have completed your booklet, swap your work with a friend and make suggestions as to how their booklet can be improved.

Dealing with sensitive information

It is important to make sure that sensitive information is kept confidential and private. This also applies to the information that is given to customers over the telephone.

While uncommon, people do make 'bogus' calls. These types of calls are usually meant to gain information from a person or organisation. In a business setting, such calls are made to get hold of information which could be of use to a competitor, for example in knowing a business's profit margin on items.

To avoid information getting into the wrong hands, companies have policies and systems in place. One of the main methods is to limit the amount of information a person can access. Normally a junior member of staff has access to less information than a more senior member of the company.

Key term

Profit margin
The amount of profit expressed as a proportion of the turnover. So if a customer buys an item for £2, which costs £1.50 to produce, the profit margin is $33\frac{1}{3}$ per cent.

Activity: Call centre

Imagine you work in a call centre. Prepare a telephone script which makes sure that you cover all data protection requirements.

Now get into pairs. Your partner should 'call' you and try to trick you into giving away sensitive information. Swap roles.

Check

- The Data Protection Act is a law which makes sure that data is stored and processed fairly and lawfully.

- Protect yourself by always following your company's procedures for dealing with sensitive or confidential information.

L02 Taking short messages

Sometimes you will need to answer a telephone call and write down a short message which needs to be passed to another member of staff. This will happen normally when the other person is on the telephone dealing with another caller or when they are out at lunch.

In order to give your colleague as much information as possible, it is important to note down:

- the date and time of the call

- the caller's name and number

- the purpose of their call, as accurately as possible.

It is also helpful to give an idea of how urgent the message is and whether or not the recipient needs to take any action.

Normally, a business will have a specially formatted note-taking pad which will look like the one below:

Phone messages

Caller's name: _____

Call taken by: _____

For the attention of: _____

Time of call: _____

Reason for call: _____

_____
_____
_____
_____
_____
_____
_____
_____

Functional skills

You will be practising your writing skills in English by taking messages carefully and accurately.

Activity: Heard it on the grapevine

1. As a group arrange yourselves in a circle. One person needs to write down a short message on a piece of paper, typically three to four lines.

2. The person must then whisper that message to the first person in the circle.

3. The last person who receives the message should then write down what they have been told on a piece of paper.

4. The two messages should then be looked at side by side to compare the spoken and written messages. Think about the questions below when comparing the messages.

- What has happened?

- Why has this happened?

- What might happen in the workplace if the same thing happened?

Activity: Taking messages

You are to role play in pairs a telephone conversation in which one of you is phoning a business to leave a short message. The other is the administrator taking the message. On an A5 piece of paper prepare a message pad like the one on page 52.

When the administrator has taken the message and completed all the points on the message pad, he or she should repeat the message back to the caller. The caller then scores the administrator marks out of 10 for the accuracy of the message. Then reverse roles.

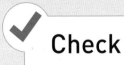

Check

- Use short messages to make sure you have captured what a person is saying in a telephone conversation.

- If you are in any doubt, ask the caller to repeat what they have said so that you can pass on an accurate message.

L03 Well-handled calls and the benefits to business

Making a good impression

The first **impression** you give a person can often be the lasting one they will have of you. The same is true when working in business administration. The difference is that you are representing the company you work for and, therefore, the impression you give represents both you and the business. The key is to know how to make a good impression.

Some of the ways this can be achieved are outlined below:

- Your **tone** of voice – if you are aggressive or miserable, the person you are talking to will get a negative impression of you and your company.

- Clarity – it is important to be clear when speaking to people on the telephone so that you do not have to repeat yourself too much, and a person fully understands what you are saying. To avoid being misunderstood, try not to use business jargon (unless you know the person you are talking to understands what you are saying). Use simple and short sentences. You may need to repeat yourself if you are clarifying instructions as this will help to avoid mistakes.

- Listening – this is a skill we take for granted. However, it takes practice to be a good or active listener. Active listening involves fully understanding the conversation while adding to what has been said. You do this by asking questions or asking for points to be repeated if they are not clear. Part of active listening is the skill of making notes while staying focused on what has been said.

- Questioning – it is said in business that it is better to not say anything than ask a 'bad' question. As with listening, asking questions is a skill that is developed with practice. It is important to understand the purpose of a telephone call and the way the conversation is going to make sure that any questions you ask add to it and do not distract from the discussion.

- Checking information when taking a message – this is a very important skill that must be used whenever you take a telephone message. You must write down exactly what the caller is saying. The message may need to be passed on and, if it is incorrect, the person will follow the instructions and end up with the wrong result.

Key terms

Impression
The image of a person that someone is left with after talking to or dealing with another person.

Tone
The way in which one person speaks to another person.

- Giving accurate and up-to-date information – when people call a company for advice or help, they expect to be given information which is both accurate and up to date. For example, in the past customers might be told that an item was in stock while in reality none was available. The customer therefore faced disappointment when they arrived to collect their goods. While this still happens, technology has improved the efficiency of tracking items and so the chances of being let down by a business have been reduced.

The benefits a good impression can bring

By presenting a good impression of an organisation, customers feel positive about dealing with the business in the future. If customers are satisfied with the service they receive, they might tell others about it and so new customers are attracted to the business.

However, if people receive a negative impression of a business, they will also pass this experience on to others and this may negatively affect the business.

Functional skills

Practising telephone conversations will help to improve your speaking and listening skills in English.

Activity: Role play

In pairs, think up five different role play telephone situations which involve a conversation with each other.

Try to choose a variety of callers and practise using different tones and language.

Check

- Practise your listening and questioning skills in order to improve.
- Only ask questions that are relevant and add to the conversation.

ASSESSMENT OVERVIEW

While working through this unit, you will have prepared for completing the following assessment tasks:

○	1.1	Identify the purpose of the call	Pages 46–47
○	1.2	Confirm the name and number of the person to be contacted before making the call	Page 46
○	1.3	Make a call communicating basic information clearly and accurately	Page 47
○	2.1	Answer the call promptly and politely, observing any organisational procedures	Page 48
○	2.2	Identify the caller, where they are calling from and the reason for their call	Pages 48–49
○	2.3	Follow any organisational procedures relating to confidentiality and security	Pages 50–51
○	2.4	Take short messages	Pages 52–53
○	3.1	State how appropriate tone and language create a positive impression	Pages 54–55
○	3.2	State how creating a positive impression during a call benefits the organisation	Pages 54–55

Assignment tips

- Your tutor may set you a role play of a telephone call for this unit. For this you will need to take on a particular role and think about how you should prepare for the call. You will also need to follow a clear process when answering a call to achieve all the grading criteria.

- In preparation for making and receiving a call, you might find it useful to draw a flow chart. This will help you to identify the different steps you need to go through and will help you pass this unit.

- You will need to state two benefits of creating a positive impression for the organisation. You may do this through a recorded conversation with your tutor.

WELCOMING VISITORS

Businesses receive all sorts of visitors – from suppliers and customers to potential employees. For many visitors, the first impression they will have of the business is the receptionist.

First impressions are important, so through this unit you will learn how to welcome visitors and create a positive impression. You will also learn why organisations feel this is such an important skill.

In this unit you will:

- Be able to welcome visitors in a positive way

- Know why it is important to an organisation that visitors are made welcome

Why do you think first impressions are so important for businesses?

Visitors

An organisation will receive any number of visitors over the course of a day. These may include:

*   members of the public

*   people from the same organisation

*   people from other organisations, such as suppliers, customers or clients.

Each of these will be visiting your organisation for a different reason.

Case study:

Chalky College

Chalky College has around 1000 students aged between 14 and 19 studying at its two campuses. The college regularly receives 20 or more visitors a day. All visitors need to sign into the visitors' book, be given a visitor badge and be met at reception by a member of staff.

Colm works on reception. He has had a long week, and is distracted by some issues outside work. A visitor comes to the reception desk and asks to speak to Amy Smyth. Colm says: 'Sorry mate, don't know her. Can't help you.'

He thinks Amy probably works at the other campus, but it would take a few minutes to find out.

Activity: First impressions count

What kind of impression would Colm have made? What if the visitor's meeting with Amy Smyth was important? What do you think Colm should have done differently?

Why do visitors come?

*   To visit an individual employee – depending on the type of organisation, this may be for a sales meeting, to discuss a new product, to agree on some details of a decision.

    These visitors will probably need to be met at reception by the employee they are visiting. So the receptionist will need to contact the employee, tell them who has arrived, and arrange for them to meet the visitor.

- For large meetings, or conferences – these may involve people from the same organisation (perhaps from different offices) and people from outside organisations (sometimes called 'delegates').

  If a meeting is particularly large, it would not be practical to have all the delegates met by individual employees. It is likely that there would be a list of people attending, and the receptionist would direct the delegates to make their own way to the meeting.

- Businesses receive a range of different deliveries – from products that have been ordered by an individual member of staff to regular postal deliveries. If an organisation is large enough to have a post room, the receptionist would probably direct most deliveries to it.

  However, if the organisation does not have a post room, the receptionist may sign for deliveries. (This is important for some deliveries as it can be used as evidence that the goods were delivered.)

  If a delivery is addressed to an individual employee, the receptionist would need to contact the employee to arrange for the delivery to be collected.

What do visitors want?

Visitors may request information. For example, a visitor may ask for a catalogue, or a contact telephone number. It is important that receptionists handle these requests effectively as these visitors may become customers or suppliers for the organisation.

If the receptionist cannot provide the information, he or she should contact someone within the organisation who is able to.

Activity: Handling visitors

As a small group, think about one organisation you all know. Try to identify all the different reasons why visitors might be calling at the organisation. What skills do you think would be important when welcoming all these different visitors? What sorts of information might the visitors need?

Check

- An organisation may receive visitors for a wide range of reasons.

- It is important that the receptionist is able to direct visitors to the right person within the organisation.

L02 The importance of making a good impression

A first impression can be a lasting one. Working in reception, you are often the first person that a potential customer, supplier or employee sees from the organisation. That means that they may form an opinion of your organisation based entirely on their first impressions of you!

Does the person in the photo make a good impression? If you had to judge the organisation they worked for by looking at this photograph, what would you say?

What makes a good impression?

Many different things can work together to make a good first impression. However, a lot of it comes down to customer service, that is the level of service and care that the visitor feels they received from the organisation.

Things that visitors may remember include:

- Polite and friendly service – did they feel welcome, or were they treated as if they were getting in the way?

- Helpful service – did the organisation go that extra mile to answer their questions, or to make their visit pleasant?

- Professional demeanour – was the receptionist professional and effective?

A good impression can help the organisation gain more business. It is worth remembering that customers will tell *one* of their friends about *good* customer service, but will tell *ten* of their friends if they have *bad* customer service.

✱ Key term

Professional demeanour
This is how someone appears in a first impression. If you are dressed smartly, are polite and helpful, and address the visitor's needs effectively, you are likely to be thought of as having a professional demeanour.

Who are you welcoming?

You are likely to welcome a wide range of different people into your organisation. These will probably include at least some of the different groups in the diagram below:

Potential employees, who may be visiting for a job interview – if your organisation is to attract the best people, it needs to give a good first impression

Clients – your customers, without them you wouldn't have a job

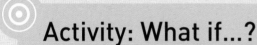

Different types of visitors

Suppliers who work with your organisation on a regular basis. The better service you provide them, the better service they will provide you

Members of the public, who may be clients or service users for your organisation

Activity: What if...?

In pairs, suggest what might happen if each of the different visitor groups above has a good first impression of the organisation.

Then suggest what might happen if they have a bad first impression.

How would this affect the organisation?

✓ Check

- Working on reception, you will be responsible for giving a good first impression of the organisation.

- A good first impression can help the organisation win new customers. A bad first impression can mean the organisation loses customers.

L01 How to welcome visitors

Your organisation is likely to have **procedures** for welcoming visitors. These should be followed closely as they can be very important – both for the security of your organisation, and for keeping an accurate list of visitors in case there is an emergency.

1. Greet visitor

When working on reception, you will be responsible for answering telephone calls, answering or forwarding emails, as well as welcoming visitors.

You should acknowledge all visitors, even if you are on the telephone. Making eye contact and showing the visitor you know they are there will create a good impression.

2. Identify reason for visit

You need to identify the reason for the visit in order to help the visitor. 'Hello, how can I help you?' is probably the most friendly and open way you could do this.

Before you can help the visitor you need to find out:

- Who they are, and what organisation they come from
- The purpose of their visit
  - o If they are visiting someone from your organisation, you need to find out who they are visiting
  - o If they are visiting for a large meeting or a conference, you need to identify which meeting they are attending in case there is more than one being held at the same time.

3. Contact appropriate person

If the visitor is there to see a particular person, you will need to contact that person to let them know their visitor is in reception.

4. Ask visitor to sign in

All visitors will need to sign a visitors' book. This will help to keep a record of who is visiting the organisation, and may also act as their **visitor's badge**. Most visitors' books record the following information:

- Name
- Organisation
- Person they are visiting
- Car registration
- Time in
- Time out.

5. Waiting

The visitor may need to wait to be met, either because they are early or because it will take a little while for the employee to get to reception. Once the visitor has signed in, you should ask them to take a seat.

If you know how long the visitor is likely to be waiting, you should tell them. They may be able to get on with some work, if they have enough time, so it's not time wasted.

Depending on the likely length of their wait, and the equipment available in reception, you might ask them if they would like a drink.

Key term

Visitor's badge
A badge or security pass, identifying the visitor.

Activity: Role play

In pairs, work through the sequence of welcoming a visitor. One of you should take Role A and the other Role B.

Role A: You are from Onyx, a local business, and visiting Bob Jenkins in marketing. Your car registration is H48 0BCZ.

Role B: You are the receptionist. Bob Jenkins is going to be in a meeting for another 15 minutes, so won't be able to collect his visitor for a little while.

Once you have worked through the role play, discuss what you thought went well. What would the visitor's first impression of the organisation be?

Functional skills

Through the activity below you will practise your **English** speaking and listening skills.

Check

- Remember to acknowledge every visitor – even if you are very busy.
- You need to make sure all visitors going into the organisation sign the visitors' book.

L01 Communicating with visitors

To work on reception, you need to have good communication skills. You also need to understand the organisation you work for, because you are likely to be asked a wide range of questions.

Routine questions

The types of question you will be asked in reception will vary depending on the kind of organisation you work for. See the list on the right.

Finding answers

If you are asked questions that you don't know the answer to, don't worry, be honest and say so. It is very rare for anyone to be able to answer every question. One of the most important skills is being able to identify someone who could.

This will mean working out the best person to ask in the organisation. To do this you will need to:

- Work out which department the question relates to

- Identify the person in that department who will either be able to provide an answer, or be able to find someone who can answer the question

- Contact them, and explain the question clearly and politely

- Either tell the visitor the answer to the question, or how long an answer is likely to take.

Case study:
Chalky College

Colm is having a better day. He is working on reception and is on the telephone to his girlfriend. He notices a visitor come in and head towards him. He makes eye contact with the visitor to acknowledge their presence. 'I've got to go, so I'll call you later,' he says to his girlfriend.

'Hello, how can I help you?' Colm says to the visitor.

'Hello, I'm from Smith's Office Supplies. Would you be able to tell me who is in charge of purchasing printer ink?'

Colm thinks hard. 'No, sorry, I don't know. However, I know someone who will know. Take a seat. This should take about five minutes.' He picks up the telephone and calls someone in another department.

Routine questions receptionists are asked

↓

Directions – to facilities, a particular building or entrance

↓

Contacts – a person who the visitor needs to speak to about a specific issue or is meeting at a particular time

↓

Sales information – such as a request for a catalogue or order form

↓

Very specific questions that you might not know the answer to – you should know who in the business will know the answer

Activity: A good impression

What kind of an impression would Colm have made? What do you think Colm did well?

Tone, language and manner

When working in reception, making a good first impression of the organisation is important. Here are some things to consider:

- Speak clearly – make sure the meaning of what you are saying is easy to understand. This is even more important if you are giving someone directions, as they may not know the office as well as you

- Be polite. Thank visitors for completing the visitors' book or handing back their visitor's pass

- Use a warm and friendly tone. Open questions like 'How can I help you?' go a long way in helping you to appear welcoming

- Remember your body language. Make eye contact with visitors. This will show that you have acknowledged them, and that you are dealing with them personally. Don't fold your arms when speaking to someone – this is called 'closed' body language and may give a negative impression

- Smile!

Activity: Design a poster

Working in small groups, produce an A3 poster giving instructions for good practice for someone working in reception. This should cover:

- How to greet a visitor and answer their questions

- What to do if you are unable to answer their questions

- Top tips for giving a good impression.

Check

- If you don't know the answer to a visitor's question, ask someone who does.

- Remember to be polite, friendly and helpful – this will give a good impression of your organisation.

ASSESSMENT OVERVIEW

While working through this unit, you will have prepared for completing the following assessment tasks:

○	1.1	Welcome visitors and establish the purpose for their visit	Pages 58–59
○	1.2	Follow organisational procedures for receiving visitors	Pages 62–63
○	1.3	Answer routine questions	Page 64
○	1.4	Make visitors feel welcome during any period of waiting	Page 65
○	1.5	Use appropriate tone and language, including body language, when dealing with visitors	Page 65
○	2.1	State how treating visitors politely and in a positive way benefits the organisation	Pages 60–61

Assignment tips

- Quite a lot of the assessment for this unit will be through practical tasks that your tutor will witness. You will need to know the agreed procedure for greeting visitors (i.e. signing the visitors' book, etc.). You will also need to be aware of your body language. Try to think about the way you sit or stand, and what it might be saying about you.

- You will need to follow two types of organisational procedure when welcoming visitors. You will also need to answer two routine questions correctly and clearly.

- You will need to identify one benefit to the organisation of treating visitors politely and in a positive way. You should try to give the reason a context. For example, you could say why the visitor might be visiting, and the effect this may have on their long-term dealings with the organisation.

When employed by a company as an administrator, you will often need to handle mail. Dealing with incoming and outgoing mail is a very important task to make sure that information is kept flowing within the business. If there are problems with the distribution of mail, then the impact on the business can be dramatic, including the possibility of losing customers.

In this unit you will:

- Know why it is important for a business to handle mail efficiently and securely

- Be able to deal with incoming mail

- Be able to deal with outgoing mail

Every day it is thought that between 60 and 80 million items of mail are sent or received. How many different reasons can you think of why a business would need to send mail?

L01 The importance of handling mail efficiently

How efficient distribution of mail benefits a business

Mail can be seen as the lifeblood of the world economy as businesses depend on information to work effectively. If there is a hiccup in the system, and mail does not get to where it is supposed to be going on time, then this can cause big problems for a company.

An efficient mail distribution system can benefit a business in many ways. First, it is important that mail is received in a timely manner. A customer would not be pleased if their order arrived at a supplier six weeks after they had placed it just because it became caught up in the internal mail system.

Second, an efficient mail system presents a professional image to customers. If a customer rings up with a query and their order can be found quickly then they will think that the company you work for is on the ball.

Case study:
Pattison and Sons Builders

Pattison and Sons is a building business run by a father and his sons. Jim Pattison is the Managing Director of the business and his sons, Russell and Richard, specialise in bricklaying and joinery. The business, which has been successful for many years, is run on a very traditional basis with very little use of modern ICT.

Due to a large increase in their workload, the father and sons team can no longer manage all the administration and building work, so they decide to employ an administrator.

After interviewing a number of candidates, Barbara is chosen. The three family members of the business are very happy with their choice of administrator and feel she will do a good job. However, Barbara has mainly dealt with email and the occasional letter at her previous employers.

It is soon clear that Barbara is starting to have problems dealing with the mail. Sometimes she forgets to invoice customers or she invoices customers incorrectly, often sending letters to the wrong address. She is also forgetting to respond to requests for payment from suppliers. Jim notices that his cash flow is not as healthy as it used to be and this concerns him greatly.

✳ Key terms

Invoice
An invoice is a document sent to customers requesting payment for the supply of goods or services.

Cash flow
Money flowing in and out of a business in the form of payments and receipts.

Activity: Group activity

As a group, consider how Barbara's mistakes are affecting the cash flow of the business. What sort of impression do you think both suppliers and customers of Pattison and Sons are getting of the business?

What could Pattison and Sons have done when Barbara started to work for the business that might have helped to avoid these problems?

Why mistakes or delays can have a negative effect

If you look back to the Pattison and Sons case study, it gives some idea of the type of problems that can happen if a person is not dealing with mail correctly. Businesses rely on getting paid for the goods or services they provide. If they do not have any money coming into the business then they cannot pay suppliers or employees' wages. It is often said in business that a company can operate while in debt but it cannot continue to trade if it has no cash flow. Also, if a business is not dealing with mail quickly, delays will give customers a negative impression as their queries may not be getting dealt with quickly. This could even lead to a customer taking their business elsewhere.

Key term

Negative impression
When a customer receives poor service and bases their future opinions of the business on that view.

Activity: Mail handling problems and their impact

Create a table which follows the same layout as the one below. An example of how the table needs to be filled in has been given.

Problem	Potential effect on business
Information not received by correct person	Information not processed on time or incorrectly processed. For example, a customer may suffer delay or receive the wrong goods.
Information is received late	
Invoices received late	
Payments to customers sent late	

Check

- Efficient mail distribution is important as it saves a company time and money.

- Internal mail is the term given to mail that is sent internally within a business.

L01 The importance of handling mail securely

Dealing with confidential information

When **dealing with mail** in a business environment you will often be handling mail that is confidential. The information could be confidential for many reasons. For example, it could contain personal details or information that is sensitive to the business which, if it falls into the wrong hands, could give competitors an advantage.

It is important to handle mail securely for a number of reasons:

1. It does not look good if an organisation keeps losing mail and customer or personal details 'leak' out. This can be very damaging to an organisation, as the general public may lose trust in them and decide to take their business elsewhere. (Over the last few years there have been several high profile cases of private data being lost or stolen.)

2. Businesses have to operate efficiently to remain competitive. If important information is slow to arrive, or gets lost, it will take longer for a job to be completed and the hold-up may cause customers concern. In the long term the company might lose customers.

The Data Protection Act

The **Data Protection Act**, 1988, is a law that was passed to control the means by which data can be stored, processed and used by businesses. The Act covers both paper-based information and information stored on a computer. Importantly, the responsibility of making sure that a person follows the Act lies with the person using the computer. This means that, if a piece of information is passed to the wrong hands, the person who gets hold of the information and passes it on could be liable if the case goes to court. The following highlight some of the key parts of the Data Protection Act:

- Data should be obtained fairly and lawfully

- Data held should not be excessive

- Data must be kept up to date

- Data must not be kept longer than needed

- An individual has the right to see any data stored about them.

Key terms

Dealing with mail
A very important operation within a business as many customers still use mail as a way of doing business. Efficient mail delivery ensures that mail does not go missing and customers receive good levels of customer service.

Data Protection Act
A law which protects the general public from having their personal data misused.

Case study:
Pattison and Sons Builders

After a couple of months it soon becomes clear that Barbara is doing more than just handling mail incorrectly. It seems that not only is the business's cash flow in trouble due to Barbara's mistakes, Pattison and Sons is also struggling to win new business.

Every time the company gives a quote for a new building job the price seems to be always mysteriously beaten. This worries Jim greatly – his company has always won business because it offers competitive quotes and work is carried out to a high standard. The next day Jim decides to investigate why his company cannot secure new business and what he finds alarms him immensely.

Follow correct procedures for delivering confidential mail

Use of appropriate postal service recorded delivery or special delivery

Ways of keeping mail confidential

Labelling post 'Confidential' or 'Confidential, not to be opened before delivery'

Use of special envelopes or postage bags

Activity: Group discussion

What do you think Barbara could be doing which is costing Pattison and Sons business? Which law is in place to protect the private information of businesses and individuals? What can Jim do now to improve the situation?

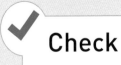

Check

- Confidential information is data that is sensitive to a business or individual.
- The Data Protection Act is a law which is designed to protect individuals and businesses from improper use of data.

L02 Dealing with incoming mail

Sorting post appropriately

The Royal Mail estimates that on average 84 million items of post are sent every day. Making sure that all the mail is delivered to the correct place is a massive job. However, that is not where it stops.

When mail is delivered to a business it must be **sorted** into the correct order so it can be sent to the correct department within the business. That may seem a simple task but a large business can receive several thousand items of post a day and so the scale of the job is very large. Despite the popularity of email, many businesses still employ staff to sort and deliver mail to the correct departments. A popular name for the area within the business in which these employees work is the 'Mail Room'. The diagram below shows the **flow of mail** through a business.

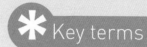

✳ Key terms

Sorting
The process of putting mail into different piles so it can be distributed to the correct department.

Flow of mail
The process which mail goes through from when it is sent until it arrives at its destination.

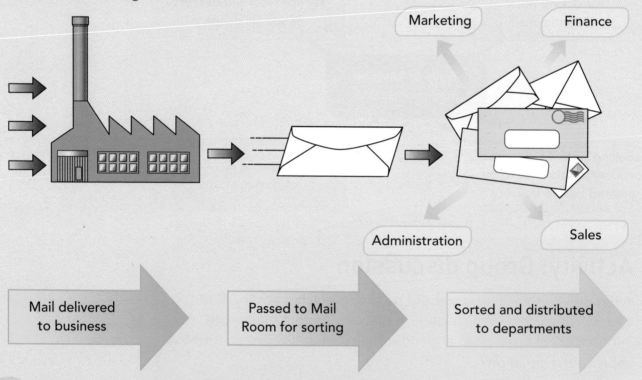

Marketing · Finance · Administration · Sales

| Mail delivered to business | Passed to Mail Room for sorting | Sorted and distributed to departments |

◎ Activity: Wrongly delivered mail

Look at the diagram above and make a list of problems that might result in mail not being distributed to the correct department.

Where do you think the problems are most likely to occur and why? Can you think of a simpler, more efficient system?

Suspicious or damaged items

When working in a mail sorting room, it is really important that you know how to look for suspicious items of post. Over the years there have been a number of times where the postal system has been used to cause harm to others. In 2001, a number of people were killed when a letter containing the bacterium Anthrax was sent through the post. Thankfully, however, such incidents are very rare indeed.

As well as suspicious items, mail room operatives must be watchful in dealing with damaged items of post. When dealing with damaged items there are a number of things you need to know.

1. You must know the procedure for dealing with damaged items.

2. Who you need to report the problem to.

3. You would normally be required to contact the sender to inform them that the item was damaged upon receipt.

4. They may need to send out a replacement or be advised that their despatch team are not sending out mail securely.

5. You would need to know the reporting/recording procedure for the receipt of damaged items.

Activity: Procedures for dealing with suspicious or damaged items

For this task you are to work in pairs. You are to imagine you work for a large organisation and have been asked to develop a new procedure for dealing with suspicious or damaged items of mail.

You need to draw up a written procedure and a flow chart of your new idea.

After you have finished developing your idea you need to present your work to your group.

Check

- Incoming mail is post that has been sent to the business and is 'incoming'.

- Suspicious or damaged items must be recorded and reported using the correct procedure so that the problem can be corrected.

L02 Distributing incoming mail

Distribute incoming mail accurately and to a deadline

Earlier we discussed the need to distribute mail efficiently and accurately. This is because, very often, a person will be expecting to receive an item of mail and they cannot make progress until this item is received.

Companies will often have in place what are known as 'service level agreements'. These documents are simply an agreement between two companies explaining what level of service they can expect to receive.

One of the standards will relate to the time allowed to deal with mail. The agreement may say for example 'all mail will be dealt with and replied to within 48 hours of receipt'. If this is the case, all mail must be processed within two working days, otherwise your employer will be breaking their agreement. This would not help your relations with a valued customer.

Making sure post is delivered to the correct person

If you work in a large organisation then it is likely that you will receive hundreds, if not thousands, of items of mail each day. Imagine also that your company employs a couple of thousand people in the office where you work. This should now give you some idea of the scale of operations that are needed to make sure post is delivered to its correct destination. Often companies follow a similar procedure to make sure that mail is sent to the correct person. This would normally work in the following way:

1. Sacks of inbound mail are dropped off at the company's mail room for sorting.

2. The mail is sorted into departmental piles (this can be done by putting the letters into named pigeon holes to keep them separate).

3. The mail may then be sorted into named employee piles.

4. The mail is delivered to the correct person by hand.

Delivering post at set times of day

Most businesses will have written policies for the handling of mail. These policies will clearly set out the time by which employees should receive mail. They usually describe the way in which post is to be delivered and precisely where in the department post is received.

Activity: Policy for dealing with incoming mail

Work individually to create a new policy for dealing with incoming mail. Your policy must include your procedures, along with timescales and actions you could take if those timescales are not met.

How could this help a business be more effective?

Activity: Service standards

Ask your tutor to arrange a visit to the administration office of your centre.

While visiting the administration office try to interview one of the administration staff about the expected service level they have to provide in dealing with post.

After you have had your visit, you need to create a poster which highlights what you have discovered.

Functional skills

If you use design or word-processing software to produce the poster, you will be practising your ICT skills.

Check

- If mail gets lost, or is not processed quickly, then customers may start to lose faith in the business.

- Dealing with mail at set times is important so that staff have a deadline to work to and customer promises can be met.

L03 Dealing with outgoing mail

Collecting post at set times

The latest time in the day that mail can be sent should be set out in the policy for handling mail.

It is important to remember that outgoing post must be collected from departments in time. It can then be collected by whichever postal service is used and delivered to its recipient in an acceptable timescale.

It is difficult otherwise for businesses to make promises to customers if employees are sending out mail at different times.

All large businesses have postal deadlines which mean that if an item of post is not ready for posting at a certain time, it will have to wait until the next day. It is not simply a case of putting all of the mail in the local postbox – in business, companies tend to use a variety of different postal services. You are going to explore these later in this unit. There may be additional tasks to do. For example, you may be required to frank mail so it can be posted. If there are hundreds of items this will take a long time. So you have to remember that the last postal collection is likely to be early in the evening and you cannot afford to miss it.

Despatching

Despatching is the term given to sending mail out by a postal service. When despatching mail there are a number of important things you have to remember. All postal services have a set way in which they like post to be addressed. They may provide labels for you to write and stick on, or even plastic postal bags in which to put your mail. However, whichever method the business uses, there are basic requirements which must be met including:

- Checking if the mail is urgent

- Identifying the type of postal service needed and arranging this through an appropriate delivery company

- Knowing the weight and size of the package (this will affect how much it will cost to deliver)

- Making sure that the package is sealed and securely packaged

- Making sure that the package is clearly and accurately addressed

- Checking that all appropriate delivery documentation is completed.

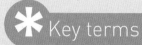
Key terms

Postal services
The term given to a range of different mail delivery companies.

Franking
The process of passing mail through a machine which franks a stamp on to it. The purpose of franking is to save time.

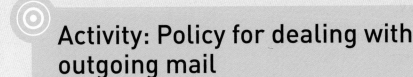

Activity: Policy for dealing with outgoing mail

Work individually to create a new policy for dealing with outgoing mail. Your policy must include your procedures, along with timescales and actions you could take if those timescales are not met.

Activity: Costing up the price of a delivery

Contact a range of delivery companies by telephone or via the Internet and find out which is the cheapest for delivery of the following package:

- Package size: 50 cm long × 30 cm wide × 15 cm deep
- Weighs 1.2 kg
- From the postcode of your centre to SW1A 1AA (find out who lives here!).

When carrying out your research complete the table below.

Name of delivery company	Name of service/features of service	Cost
Parcelforce	Express 9 – guaranteed by 9 a.m. next working day	£29.50

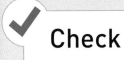

Check

- Accurate despatching of mail is important otherwise it may get sent to the wrong person. This would cause delay and possibly some embarrassment to the business.

- It is important to use the right delivery service for the needs of the business. When thinking about a courier, cost and delivery times must be considered.

ASSESSMENT OVERVIEW

While working through this unit, you will have prepared for completing the following assessment tasks:

edexcel

Assignment tips

- Remember that 'efficient' means that mail is delivered on time and to the correct person. You need to state two ways in which this benefits the business.

- You need to provide two examples to show why inaccuracies or delays can have a negative impact.

- You need to provide two examples to identify procedures to protect confidential information.

- A number of the assessment tasks for this unit will be practical. When you are being observed for assessment, it is very important that you can be seen to go through all the checks that you need to complete. It might be a good idea to talk through the task you are completing as you are observed so your tutor can understand your thought processes.

CREATING BUSINESS DOCUMENTS

When working in administration you will be faced with a wide variety of business documents. As part of your role, you need to both create and handle many different types of business documents accurately and efficiently. This means you need to know when it is appropriate to use a template and house style, as well as understanding what communication style you should use.

In this unit you will:

- Know that there are different types of business document

- Know why it is important to use the right communication style in business documents

- Be able to produce routine business documents

Why do you think it is important to understand the different types of documents you will use as an administrator?

L01 Different types of business documentation

Effective communication is important for the smooth running of a business. People within the organisation need to be able to choose and use appropriate business documents to communicate information internally and to those outside.

They can also be used to give instructions, attract potential customers and confirm agreements. You will learn about the different documents used for these purposes later in the unit.

Case study:

The Moorcroft Hotel

The Moorcroft is an exclusive 5-star hotel in Leeds that boasts an 18-hole championship golf course and a luxury health spa. It opened in 1990. In late 2009 it became clear that membership numbers had almost halved and hotel room bookings had reduced by 35 per cent.

Director of Operations Charlie Statham took on the task of uncovering the reasons for the decline. She found that instead of membership subscription reminders being sent out by letter, they were using email to save postage costs. However, many of the customers' email addresses were wrong or out of date, and the reminders were getting caught in customers' junk mail filters.

Activity: Group discussion

As a group, discuss what you think Charlie Statham should do to solve the problems at The Moorcroft Hotel. Think about how long-standing members may have felt if they believed the business had just ignored them. How might this have affected the business? How could Charlie ensure this could never happen again?

Sending documents

As shown in the case study about The Moorcroft Hotel, businesses need to choose carefully how to communicate information through business documents. Choosing how to send a business document is important in order to make sure the information gets to the right person in an effective format. Some of the most common delivery options for communicating business information and the purpose of each document are in the table below.

Document type	Purpose of document
Letter	• Letters can be formal. • Letters are used to communicate with people and organisations outside your business. • Letters come in many forms. Their main purpose is normally to advise a business, customer, supplier or business contact that an event has happened or is about to happen or to confirm agreements and contracts.
Memo	• A memo (full name *memorandum*) is a document used within a business to inform employees that an event is about to happen. • Memos are not usually written in the same formal manner as letters.
Emails	• Email is a now very popular as it is quicker and cheaper to send complicated documents than traditional 'snail' mail (i.e. letters). It is now one of the most common methods of business communication. • Email can be used for many purposes including communicating with customers, suppliers, colleagues and other business contacts.
Faxes	• Faxes were a popular method of communication before email became widely used. • Faxes are still in use today and have the benefit of letting exact copies of documents (handwritten) be sent to another person in a different place.

Activity: Sending documents

Imagine you are applying for a job at The Moorcroft Hotel. For this activity you are to apply in writing for the post of 'Hotel Receptionist'. Your letter of application must be professional in terms of content and the way it looks. You then have to create an address for The Moorcroft Hotel and finally prepare an envelope for the letter.

Check

- It is important to think about how business documents will be sent. How can you make sure the information gets to the right person?

- Some business documents are only used within an organisation, while others can be used for colleagues, customers, suppliers, etc.

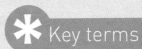

Key terms

Business documents
Documents either in paper or electronic form which are used in business for a number of different purposes. For the document to be useful, it must be completed with accuracy.

Purpose of document
Each type of document performs a specific function. It is important that the correct document is used for the correct process if an administrative system is to work efficiently.

L01 Uses of business documents

Businesses use a variety of types of document, each of which has a very specific purpose. The following two tables describe the most common types of document you are likely to come across while working as an administrator and also the purpose of each document.

The first table (below) describes business documents used in meetings and to advertise a company. The second table (on the right) describes documents used by businesses to order, pay for and deliver items.

Document type	Purpose of document
Agenda	An agenda is a document that is used to advise workers what is going to be discussed at a meeting. Agendas are always written in the same format and include the following: • Name of person who called meeting • Type of meeting • Time, date and venue of meeting • List of attendees • Apologies for absence (list of people who cannot attend) • Matters arising from previous meeting • Items to be discussed • Any other business (AOB) • Date and time of next meeting. An agenda should be sent out in good time before a meeting so that if attendees need to carry out research for the meeting they have time to do so.
Minutes	Minutes are a formal record of what has been discussed at a meeting. Normally a secretary or nominated person will be asked to attend and write up the minutes of a meeting.
Reports	Reports are formal documents which bring together and summarise the findings of research or information that is important for a business. Reports are often used to present information on sales figures.
Promotional flyers	Promotional flyers are used to advertise a product, service or event. Flyers come in many designs and sizes but are usually bold and colourfully designed. A flyer will contain logos and images of what is being advertised.

Document type	Purpose of document
Order forms	An order form is a document that is used to order items from a business or supplier. Order forms are laid out in a very clear manner and will include sections to enter the following information: • Address of supplier • Date of order • Order number • Description of item • Item code • Quantity of item needed • Cost(s) of items ordered • Total cost of order • VAT • Total cost of order including VAT. It is common for order forms to be transmitted electronically by Electronic Data Interchange (EDI) or more often by email. Both the purchaser and supplier will keep records of orders sent so they can make sure they send and receive the correct items.
Delivery notes	A delivery note is a document that is usually attached to an item when it is in the process of being delivered. The delivery note contains information about what the package contains. It is useful for warehouse workers so they can check off the items that have been sent against what is in the package.
Invoices	An invoice is a request for payment that is usually sent out between 30 and 90 days after an order has been sent. Invoices contain the following information: • Invoice number • Name and address of customer • Description and quantity of items being invoiced for • Total invoice amount • VAT • Total invoice amount including VAT • Payment terms.

Activity: Presentation

For this task you will work in pairs to create a presentation that highlights different business document types and their purposes.

You may choose to base your presentation on one of the following:

- Documents used in meetings (e.g. to present sales briefings or research findings)

- Documents used when ordering items (e.g. to order paper and stationery or other products).

Check

- Business documents help businesses operate efficiently as they each have a specific purpose. Using the correct type of document avoids confusion.

- Business documentation must have a clear and appropriate layout, otherwise it is easy for the user to make mistakes.

L01 Document templates and
L02 language

Templates

Business templates are used for many reasons including speed (i.e. making it possible to create documents quickly), accuracy and efficiency. Templates allow a business to create a set of documents that can be edited as necessary.

Templates are ready-made documents that are saved on a business's computer network. Each document has areas that are protected. This means that there are sections which cannot be changed and so they stay accurate and **consistent** every time the document is printed out. However, the document also includes areas that can be edited so it can fit with the needs of the user.

Key term

Consistent
If something is consistent, it remains the same or largely unchanged.

> **Consistency** – using templates means documents all look similar, making them more professional

> **The benefits of using templates**

> **Time-saving** – templates help employees create business documents

> **Clarity** – templates help make sure all important information is included

Activity: Use a template

Using the Internet (or a document that your tutor has provided) find an example of a template for one of the business documents listed on pages 82–83. Print the document and make notes on it to identify the areas where an employee would need to input information.

Try to identify which information would be the same each time the document was created and which information would need to be updated each time.

Using the correct communication style in business documentation

It is important to understand when it is appropriate to use informal and formal communication style. Different stakeholders will expect to be addressed in different ways. For example, an employee would use formal language when writing a letter to a senior manager in another business, but may use informal language when communicating with a colleague.

It is usual practice to use formal language when communicating with people outside your company. This is because formal language presents a professional image of the business you work for. You should use formal language when communicating with a senior manager from your organisation, because they will expect you to be precise and clear.

Formal communication

When should you use formal or informal communication?

Talking to your peers in the same department

Contacting external customers

Contacting senior managers

Informal communication

Confirming payment

Dealing with customer queries

Talking to team members for social purposes

Activity: Formal and informal language

Imagine you are an administrator for a busy company. Draft a 200-word memo asking the staff for their comments on the postal distribution service. In pairs share your memos and try to distinguish between formal and informal language.

* Key terms

Informal communication
Communication which uses 'everyday' language and is not kept on record for future reference.

Formal communication
Communication which uses professional language and where a record is kept for future reference.

Stakeholder
Anybody with some form of interest in a business who stands to lose if it is run badly.

✔ Check

- Document templates save you time and help present a more consistent image.
- Generally, formal language is best used when communicating with external customers and senior staff.

L02 House style

A house style is a set of guidelines produced by a business for the appearance of its documents. It might include the following:

- Rules for how the company should use its logos

- Guidelines on which fonts should be used in documents

- Notes on how employees should spell certain words.

The house style helps keep the style of an organisation's documents consistent (even though employees will be creating many different documents) and presents a more consistent, professional image.

A good house style should be well thought out and will reflect the type of organisation it is being used for. For example, many water utility companies use the colour blue in their logos and communications.

Activity: What does the logo say?

Research a number of well-known company logos. Draw and complete a table like the example below explaining the design of each logo.

Business logo	Explain why you think the logo has been designed in the way it has and what the impact of the design will be on the company's house style
E.g. **SPANDAS**	The logo for the supermarket SPANDAS has been designed so that the name of the business is the first thing you see. The colours have been chosen because they provide a clear contrast which is readable to people who may have sight difficulties: white writing on a red background. The logo is clear and simple. The supermarket aims for the image to reflect the way they want customers to feel about shopping with them (that they provide a simple and easy way to shop).

Writing appropriate routine documents

When working in business administration you will be expected to produce documents that will be sent to people outside your organisation. Accurate spelling, punctuation and grammar are very important, as is the correct opening and complimentary close. Also, select the correct type of communication for the message you are trying to get across.

Things to avoid when writing business communications

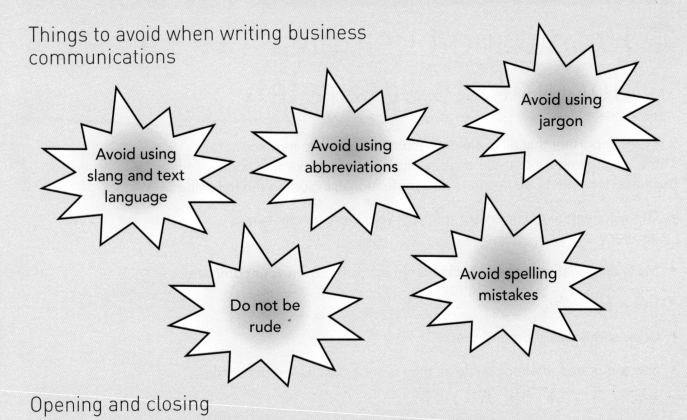

Avoid using slang and text language

Avoid using abbreviations

Avoid using jargon

Do not be rude

Avoid spelling mistakes

Opening and closing

When writing a letter or email to an individual, there may be times when you know the name and title of the individual and other times when you do not. There are some rules you need to remember when writing formal letters or emails.

	Appropriate greeting	Complimentary close
If you know the individual's name and/or title	Dear Jane OR Dear Mrs Smith	Yours sincerely
If you do not know the individual's name	Dear Sir/Madam	Yours faithfully

Activity: Writing a house style guide

Draw up a house style guide for openings and closings to be used in different circumstances for an organisation that you know.

Check

- A house style can be used to present information consistently and make decisions about fonts, colours, logos, etc.

L03 Producing business documents accurately

It is very important that all business documents are prepared accurately. There are a number of simple ways in which you can make sure your business documents are accurate and professional, including the following:

- Get a colleague or supervisor to check your work for clarity and accuracy

- Make sure that your spell checker is set up correctly on your computer

- Use a dictionary

- Keep sentences short and simple

- Use templates where possible as they reduce the chance of mistakes.

Activity: The Moorcroft Hotel

After Charlie Statham carried out her investigation into why golf and leisure membership numbers had gone down, she found out that much of the documentation used by the business was not fit for purpose. She has decided to review and change the format and content of the documents currently being used.

For this task you are going to:

1. Look again at the different business documents in the tables on pages 82–83 and make sure you understand their purpose.

2. Research the designs and formats of other companies' documents, including their letter headings and logos, to give you some ideas.

3. Produce new designs for all the documents you think The Moorcroft uses.

4. Make sure you think about what kind of business it is and the image it wants to create.

5. Design a new company logo.

Activity: Proofreading

Charlie Statham has drafted a letter to her customers to apologise for the lack of communication from The Moorcroft over the last year and to invite them all to a free health spa event. She has used Miss J. Jonas as the example in her letter. It is important that Charlie's letter is accurate so that the company maintains a professional image.

Read through the letter and proofread it for accuracy and spelling.

> Misses J. Jonas   The Moorcroft
> 32 Acacia Avenue   Morcroft Hall
> Middlesburn   Middlesburn
> West Yorkshire   West Yorkshire
> WY25 5RF   WY12 8DR
>   T: 0113 8941414
>
> 2/5/2011
>
> Der Mrs. Jona
>
> RE: Free health spa event
>
> I am writing to apologse for our lack of comunication with you over the last 12 months. To rward you as I loyal customer I would like to ivite you to attend our free health spa event on the 22nd May 2011. If you would like to attend ring the phone number above and simply book your plce. I hope you can atend the event and I look forward to meeting you.
>
> Yours faithfully,
>
> Charlie Statham
> Director of Operations.

Check

- Remember that all business documents give people an impression of the business that sent them.

- You need to check your work to make sure it is accurate and professional.

ASSESSMENT OVERVIEW

While working through this unit, you will have prepared for completing the following assessment tasks:

○	1.1	Identify different types of business document and when they might be used	Pages 80–83
○	1.2	State why templates are used for some business documents	Page 84
○	2.1	Give examples of when to use a formal or informal communication style	Page 85
○	2.2	State why some businesses adopt a 'house style' for certain documents	Page 86
○	3.1	Produce routine business documents using the appropriate communication style	Pages 86–87
○	3.2	Check documents for accuracy	Pages 88–89

edexcel :::

Assignment tips

- Identify four different documents. You might find it useful to explain what they would be used for in business by 'telling a story' through the documents. For example, if a business sends a document to a customer, what do they get back and what happens next?

- Give two examples of when to use a formal communication style and two examples of when to use an informal communication style. Try to explain why this communication style is suitable for each example.

- Produce three routine documents, which should include two different types of document. You can produce two versions of the same type of document, but you need to produce a different type of document for your third example.

RECORDING BUSINESS TRANSACTIONS

As an administrator you may be working in a job where you have responsibility for recording the flow of money in and out of a business. In this unit you will learn about the most frequently used financial recording documents. In order for a business to operate successfully these documents should be completed accurately and in a timely fashion.

In this unit you will:

- Know the documents used to record business transactions

- Be able to complete an order form for office supplies

Why do you think it is important to complete financial documents accurately?

L01 Documents used to record business transactions

It is important you understand that each **financial document** mentioned in this unit has a very specific purpose. The first set of documents we are going to look at are used when a company buys and sells items.

The recording of these **transactions** helps the business to keep track of its cash flow. Imagine cash flow being like the blood supply in a person's body – cash flow keeps a business alive. If a business has more money going out than coming in, it will not be able to survive for very long.

Case study:
Williamson's Music

Williamson's Music is a music production company based on the outskirts of Preston, Lancashire. The business is owned and run by Mark Williamson.

The business has been running for eight years. In that time it has not made huge profits but just enough for Mark to get by on.

The business specialises in creating and remixing music for the underground club scene. While the business is Mark's only source of income, he has treated it more like a hobby than his only source of a wage.

In common with the philosophy of this type of music industry, Mark will produce work for artists and either not charge them for it or forget to do so. His accounts are out of date and in an awful mess. Recently, times have been hard for Mark so he has decided that he must formalise the way he runs his business if it is to survive.

 Key terms

Financial documents
Specific documents that are used to record the buying and selling of goods.

Transaction
The process of paying or receiving money for goods that have been bought or sold.

Activity: Group discussion

What financial problems might Mark be facing by running the business in the way he currently does? What sort of advice do you think an accountant might give Mark about organising his finances better? How would this advice help Mark in the future?

Activity: Williamson's Music

Mark Williamson has asked for your help. He realises that if he is going to make money from his business he will need a professional set of financial documents.

You will have to produce, individually, each of the documents mentioned in the table on the following pages. You will design a logo and make sure that the layout and content of each document is accurate.

To complete this task you will have to do some research on the Internet to get a feel for each document. You can also refer back to *Unit 19 Creating business documents* (pages 86–89) for help with this activity.

Functional skills

Through finding information on the Internet for this activity you will be practising your **ICT** skills.

Petty cash

Petty cash is the term given to the small amount of money a business may keep in its office to buy small items. It is very important for a business to keep a small sum of petty cash (normally no more than £100) as certain items need to be bought to keep the business running efficiently. Such items include stationery, stamps and refreshments. However, even though the amounts spent may only be small, it is still very important that it is accounted for. For this reason, most businesses will have petty cash receipts and a recording procedure.

Recording petty cash purchases

The flow diagram on the right gives an example of how a business may record its purchases from petty cash.

Item is bought from a shop. A receipt is issued for the value of the item.

Activity: Recording petty cash

The flow diagram shows a very simple petty cash recording procedure. You now need to create a new petty cash procedure for Williamson's Music.

Receipt is passed to person in charge of petty cash. They will complete a petty cash voucher for that receipt.

Check

- Each financial document mentioned in this unit has a very specific purpose.
- It is very important to account for the spending of petty cash.

Petty cash voucher and receipt should be kept together and will then be entered in the accounts of the company.

The main financial documents used for buying and selling goods are shown in the following table. Use the information to help you with the case study and activities on the previous pages.

Name of document	Purpose of document
Purchase order	Purchase orders are used when a business wants to buy goods or services. Purchase orders are usually completed by a person with some authority and contain the following details: • Company name • Company address • Contact numbers/email address • VAT registration number (if VAT registered) • Order number • Supplier reference • Order date • Quantity/ description/item code number/unit price of goods • Signature and date of person in authority.
Delivery note	A delivery note comes with a delivery when it is received by a business. Two copies of a delivery note are usually sent and one copy is kept by the customer while the other is sent back to the supplier. The delivery note lists what has been delivered. This allows the receiving company to check if the correct items have been received, the correct quantity has been sent and if they were received on time and in good condition. The delivery note will contain the following information: • Supplier name and address • Customer name and address • VAT registration number (if VAT registered) • Contact numbers/email address/website address • Despatch date • Order number • Customer account number • Invoice number • Quantity/description/item code number/unit price of goods • Delivery date • Signature and date.
Goods received note (GRN)	A goods received note is a document which is completed internally within a business. It is usually completed by the person or department (usually the warehouse) who received the goods. The GRN provides a double check that the goods have been received on time and in good condition. The GRN will also indicate the supplier name and details. After completion a copy is sent to the accounts department and this will trigger off payment for the goods. A GRN will contain the following information: • Supplier name and address • Name of haulage/courier company • Date the GRN was written out • Name of person who checked stock • Order number • Quantity ordered/quantity delivered/description of goods • Indication of whether or not goods were received in an acceptable condition.

Name of document	Purpose of document
Invoice	An invoice is a document that is used to request payment from a customer for goods or services that have been supplied. It is important that invoices are prepared correctly otherwise a customer may become upset if they are charged too much or, alternatively, your business will lose out on profit if goods are not invoiced for correctly. An invoice will contain the following information: • Name and address of company sending invoice • Name and address of company being invoiced • Contact details/email address/website address • VAT number (if VAT registered) • Order number • Customer account number • Date and tax point • Invoice number • Item codes/quantities being invoiced for/description of items/unit price/ total unit price/invoice total/VAT element/total amount due • Payment terms.
Credit note	A credit note is used when a business has been overcharged for goods and services. In effect, a credit note is like a refund for being overcharged. There are a number of reasons why a credit note might be issued including: • Wrong prices quoted by supplier • Invoice incorrectly sent out • Wrong or damaged goods sent and customer returning goods ordered. A credit note will contain the following information: • Name and contact details of supplier • Contact details/email address/website address • VAT number (if VAT registered) • Name and address of customer • Invoice number • Credit note number • Item code of product being overcharged for • Quantity of items • Description of items • Unit price/net value/total cost/VAT/total amount being refunded • Reason for return.
Remittance advice slip	A remittance advice slip is usually attached to the invoice and makes payment easier for the customer and supplier. Traditionally, a remittance advice slip accompanies the payment which is sent by the customer to the supplier. However, technology has now made it more straightforward for payments to be made electronically straight into a supplier's bank account. In some ways this has reduced the use of a remittance advice slip.
Cheque	A cheque is a form of payment which is sent from the customer to the supplier. In completing a cheque a customer writes the following on it: • Amount in words • Date of cheque • Amount in figures • Signature (usually someone in authority). The cheque will contain additional printed details such as cheque number, branch sort code and account number and the address of the business's bank branch. Cheques are likely to be phased out by 2018 and will cease to be legal tender.
Receipt	A receipt is a document which advises the customer that their payment has been received and processed. Businesses keep receipts so they can check them against their bank statements to ensure they tally. Businesses also need them for tax purposes when filling in their end of year accounts.

L02 Complete an order form for office supplies

It is important to remember that a business must keep a close eye on its finances. Even small items which cost very little start to add up if bought on a regular basis. For this reason most companies have a procedure which must be followed before an order is placed. This allows the business to control its spending by carefully planning what it needs to spend its money on. However, a business cannot operate without supplies and therefore, at some stage, orders have to be placed.

Planning to place an order

The flowchart below provides an idea of the process a business goes through when it is planning to place an order.

Complete a purchase order form accurately

It is very important that purchase order forms are filled out accurately. It may be that a customer is waiting for the goods that you are ordering and, if they do not arrive on time or as requested, the customer will feel let down and possibly not buy from you again. There are a number of common mistakes that occur on purchase order forms including:

- Ordering the wrong item
- Entering the wrong product code
- Ordering the wrong quantity
- Describing the product incorrectly
- Inserting an incorrect unit price
- Calculating unit and total costs incorrectly.

There is an example of a purchase order form on the page opposite.

Stock checking

Check how much stock the business currently has

▼

To buy or not to buy?

Decide if an order needs placing
If, yes then

▼

Obtaining stock details

Find out the stock code, description and price details of items required

Complete a purchase order or pass to a staff member who has the authority to do so

▼

Sending purchase order

Send a copy of the purchase order to the customer and another copy to the accounts department of your employer

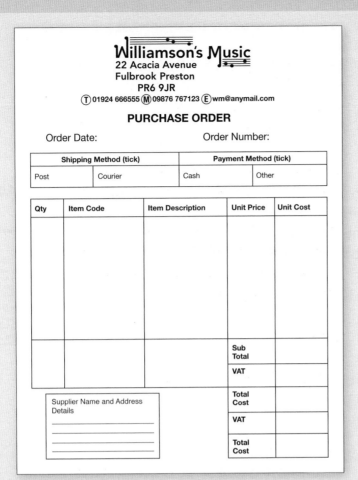

Functional skills

This activity will help you practise your Mathematics skills.

Activity: Williamson's Music order

For this task you need to complete an order for the following items for Williamson's Music. Mark requires the following items:

- 3 x 50 pack of recordable CDs = £4.99 each
- 20 x pack of CD labels = £1.99 each
- 6 x pack of CD boxes = £2.65 each
- 1 x microphone = £109.99

You need to work out VAT at 17.5 per cent and the order is to be sent to:

J & S Music Supplies
Pendle Street, Settle
North Yorkshire BD25 8ES

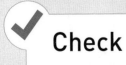

Check

- Always be 100 per cent accurate when completing purchase orders as mistakes can be very costly.
- Always check that you definitely need items before ordering them to avoid wasting company money.

Delivery notes, invoices, cheques and receipts

Delivery notes

As mentioned earlier, delivery notes are completed by the seller and tell the buyer what is being delivered. An example of a basic delivery note is shown here.

Williamson's Music
22 Acacia Avenue
Fulbrook Preston
PR6 9JR
(T) 01924 666555 (M) 09876 767123 (E) wm@anymail.com
DELIVERY NOTE

Delivered To:		Delivery note no: 765
SR Music Smith Street Cardiff CF12 7ER		Delivery method: Courier Your order: SR234 Order Date: 19/4/2011

Stock code	Quantity supplied	Item Description
4312	14 sets	Earphones

Received by: _____   Date: _____

Invoices

An invoice is a request from a seller for money that is owed. It is important that it is accurate as a mistake could lead to the seller paying the wrong amount. This may lead to the company going elsewhere for goods in the future. An example of a basic invoice is shown here.

Williamson's Music
22 Acacia Avenue
Fulbrook Preston
PR6 9JR
(T) 01924 666555 (M) 09876 767123 (E) wm@anymail.com
INVOICE

Invoice To:		Invoice Number: 001345
SR Music Smith Street Cardiff CF12 7ER		Order Number: SR234 Order Date: 19/4/2011 Payment Terms = 60 Days

Qty	Product Code	Description	Price	Total Price	Discount	Net Price
14	MP68	Microphone	109.99	1539.86	15%	1308.88

Order Value	1308.88
VAT 17.5%	229.05
Total Cost	1537.93

Cheques

A cheque is a legal document which, when completed by a person or business, forms an instruction to make payment for goods or services. In recent years, personal cheques have become less popular due to safer and more efficient electronic banking card services.

However, in business cheques are still a popular method of payment. This is because, unlike other methods, the money does not leave a bank account straightaway. It normally takes five days for a cheque to clear which means extra interest on the money the business has deposited with a bank. An example of a cheque is shown here.

Supplier receipts

The receipt is probably the most familiar document of all when looking at financial documents. A receipt provides proof of purchase and can be used for returning items or obtaining refunds if they are faulty. Businesses use receipts in much the same way as consumers do – the only difference is they will retain them for tax purposes to calculate VAT.

Activity: Analysing receipts

Collect as many receipts as you can over the period of a week and bring them into your centre. Compare the different layouts. Now make a collage out of the receipts. Make sure you label the different parts of the receipt.

Check

- It is important that invoices are paid on time otherwise this may affect the cash flow of the business that has supplied you. Companies can also charge extra for overdue invoices.

- Despite cheques being a very old payment method they are still popular because they are easy to write and secure, which means they can be sent through the post without risk. However, cheques are expected to be phased out in 2018.

ASSESSMENT OVERVIEW

While working through this unit, you will have prepared for completing the following assessment tasks:

○	1.1	Identify the types and purpose of documents used to record business transactions	Pages 92–95
○	2.1	Make plans to order appropriate supplies for a given situation	Page 96
○	2.2	Complete a purchase order form accurately	Pages 96–97
○	2.3	Receive the supplies and the delivery notes	Page 98
○	2.4	Receive the invoice from the suppliers	Page 98
○	2.5	Make out the cheque to pay the invoice	Page 99
○	2.6	Receive the supplier's receipt for payment of the invoice	Page 99

Assignment tips

- Try to include an example of when each document might be used to help show what it is used for.

- It is likely that you will complete the documents used to order office supplies. You will then be asked questions about what you have done, so it is important to know the purpose and features of each transaction.

- Try to get into the habit of giving reasons for answers, so every statement (for example, 'I used a cheque') is followed with the word 'because'.

SUPPORTING BUSINESS MEETINGS

When working in administration you will often need to organise and support business meetings. The task of arranging meetings has to be undertaken professionally and requires many skills. If a meeting is badly organised it can give a poor impression of an organisation and for that reason is a very important job. This unit will give you an introduction to the skills you need to arrange successful business meetings.

In this unit you will:

- Know what is required to hold a business meeting

- Be able to set up a room for a meeting

- Be able to support a meeting

- Be able to complete follow-up activities after a meeting

Why do you think it is important for businesses to have well-organised meetings?

L01 What is required to hold a successful business meeting?

Across the world, throughout every minute of the day, meetings at businesses will be taking place. Meetings form an important part of a business's success. Without them, important plans would not get discussed and employers would not have a clear picture of how to improve and move their businesses forward. However, a meeting is only as good as the planning that has gone into it. There is a famous saying you might want to keep in mind when organising meetings: 'fail to prepare – prepare to fail'.

Successful meetings do not just happen – they are planned for. Throughout this unit you will learn the skills needed to host successful meetings.

Case study:
Sprite & Co

Sprite & Co is a small manufacturing company based in North Yorkshire. The business is owned and run by Louise Sprite and her two children, Mary and Charlie. The company also employs 15 other staff in a range of production and administration roles.

The business specialises in making expensive equipment for the medical industry. The products have to be made to very high standards in a very clean environment. The company is a leader in its field and has been for the last ten years.

However, due to tightening budgets and cheaper imports from Asia, the business is starting to struggle. Recently a series of very important meetings has been arranged with a number of NHS trusts who are interested in buying a new piece of equipment. If Sprite & Co could secure the contracts, then the future of the business would be safe for the next five years. Louise has asked her Head of Administration, Jane Tapp, to take responsibility for organising the meetings.

Activity: Group discussion

Discuss the things Jane Tapp must think about before arranging the NHS meetings.

Why is it important for Jane to think about the factors you have identified? What might be the consequences of overlooking these factors?

Requirements of hosting a meeting

The table below shows a number of points that have to be considered before arranging a meeting. A few examples have been given:

Requirement to be considered	Reason for considering	Consequence of not considering
Number of participants	So that all the arrangements will be suitable, e.g. enough chairs, delegate packs, refreshments, etc.	There may not be enough space/resources for all the participants
Informing attendees of the date of meeting	So attendees know when the meeting is going to happen	Nobody will arrive for the meeting
Advising time and venue of meeting	So attendees arrive on time and know where to go	Late arrivals will interrupt the meeting
Providing pre-meeting reading	So attendees know what the meeting is about and what they are expected to say	The meeting will take longer and will not be as informative
Arranging refreshments	To make attendees feel comfortable in the meeting	Attendees will get restless and the meeting may become disrupted

Activity: Group discussion

Some meetings need to be held in-house while it might be better to hold others off-site. Can you think of the advantages and disadvantages for either location for different types of meeting?

Check

- Meetings are important for businesses so that they can plan for the future and staff are informed of jobs that need to be completed.

- People who attend meetings are known as **delegates** or attendees.

Key term

Delegate
Someone attending a meeting. This person may represent another business.

L01 Types of meeting

Not all meetings are the same. For example, a meeting that is being held to arrange a staff social event will be much less formal than a meeting which is attended by the board of directors of a business.

An easy way to remember the difference between a formal meeting and an informal meeting is that records are always kept of a formal meeting. This is because they may contain important information that needs to be referred back to at a later date. Also, whenever a meeting takes place between the company you work for and an outside person or business, this is usually a formal meeting.

However, meetings do not always happen at the place where you work – they may take place at another venue and this is known as an off-site meeting. If a meeting does go ahead at the place where you work, and only involves employees from your company, this is known as an in-house meeting.

Other types of informal meetings might include:

- Team briefings
- Staff training.

Documentation required for meetings

As mentioned earlier, meetings must be well planned if they are to run successfully. Part of the planning involves making sure that the correct business documentation is in place for the meeting. Examples of the types of documentation that need to be considered when planning and hosting a meeting are shown here and on the opposite page.

An agenda is a document which lists the items to be discussed at a meeting.

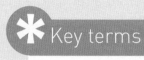
✳ Key terms

Formal meetings
A meeting between senior staff or a business and their suppliers or customers. Records are always kept.

Informal meetings
Often a meeting between colleagues. Records are rarely kept.

Agenda
An agenda is a document that is sent to attendees before a meeting to let them know what is going to be discussed.

AGENDA
Sprite & Co

New Technology Group meeting
Room 1 at 10 a.m. – 18 April 2011

---

1. Apologies for absence
2. Minutes of previous meeting
3. Matters arising
4. New technology
5. New technology training
6. Any other business (AOB)
7. Date and time of next meeting

Called by: Jane Tapp
30 March 2011

Here are some sample **minutes** from a meeting. These are a record of what has been agreed at a meeting and by whom.

Other documentation that may be used

As well as the agenda and minutes, and depending on the location and type of meeting, it would normally be appropriate to send a notification of the date and time of the meeting to attendees along with any presentation or notes required to support the meeting.

Sprite & Co.

Minutes of meeting – New Technology Group – 18 April 2011

Present: Jane Tapp (JT), Rob Jones (RJ), James Pratt (JP), Bob Johns (BJ), Nusrat Khan (NK)

1. **Apologies for absence:** Jenny Smith, Andrew Taylor.
2. **Minutes of previous meeting:** Accepted as correct and true.
3. **Matters arising:** Cost of new technology higher than costed for.
4. **New technology:** RJ discussed project managing the new technology – his suggestion was accepted by JP, BJ and NK.
5. **New technology training:** BJ and NK suggested off-site training, although it was agreed by all that in-house training would be better.
6. **Any other business:** BJ agreed to research suitable training providers for the new technology training.
7. **Date and time of next meeting:** 18 October 2011, 10 a.m.

Activity: Typing up an agenda

Jane Tapp from Sprite & Co has delegated to you the task of typing up an agenda for one of the forthcoming NHS meetings, so it must be complete and accurate.

The agenda has to include the following information:

- Keeping costs manageable
- New reporting structures
- The proposed structure of NHS contracts
- Service level the NHS can expect from Sprite & Co.

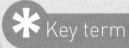

Key term

Minutes
Minutes are a formal record of a meeting which highlight what has been agreed and who is taking responsibility for completing a particular task.

Check

- Meetings can be formal or informal, depending on their purpose. Records must always be kept of a formal meeting.

- Documentation for a formal meeting should include an agenda and the minutes, along with any supporting information such as notification of the date and time of the meeting and presentation notes.

LO2 Set up a room for a meeting

For meetings to be successful and worthwhile, delegates must have all the required documents and paperwork for the meeting. When a person attends a meeting they will receive a pack which contains items such as an agenda, copies of electronic presentation slides and booklets, etc.

If the meeting is going to be a large conference-style one, hosting hundreds of delegates, then the creation of delegate packs can be a massive job and cannot be left to the last minute. The table below highlights a number of other key considerations when setting up a room.

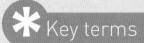
Key terms

Delegate pack
Information given to delegates which is designed to support the meeting.

Setting up a room
The process of making sure that rooms are set up and fit for the purpose of the meeting.

Consideration	Why is this consideration important?
Confirming refreshments for meeting	Meetings can last for a long time. It is usual practice to place bottles of water at the very least on delegate tables. Sometimes, the bottled water will be accompanied by mints or boiled sweets. Providing this type of refreshment allows delegates to concentrate, particularly if it is a long meeting.
Confirming consumables, for example, cups/pens, etc.	Make sure that enough items have been provided for the number of delegates attending. If delegates have bottled water on their tables, then you need to supply them with enough cups or glasses. Similarly, it is usual to provide delegates with pens when they attend meetings. Therefore, you must ensure there are enough available for each person.
Timing of refreshments	The timing of refreshments is important because delegates may become restless if they have to wait too long for a drink or something to eat. If refreshments are given too early, the flow of the meeting may be disrupted.
Equipment	It is important to check that all necessary equipment is available and working for presenters. It is very unprofessional to begin a meeting and then start setting up your equipment halfway through. A presenter nowadays would expect the following to be available in a meeting room: data projector, flip chart, pens, adequate power supplies and a means to adjust the lighting in the room.
Room temperature	This is often forgotten but the temperature of a room can affect the success of a meeting. You must remember that the temperature of a room will increase with the number of delegates attending. It is important that the room is not too hot or delegates will start to feel uncomfortable and begin to doze. If a room is too cold it will also limit the amount of useful work that can be completed as delegates will not be able to concentrate on what is being discussed.

Order of performing tasks

It is important that you follow a procedure when setting up a room for a meeting, otherwise problems may occur. The chart below shows a basic procedure that could be followed to make sure the meeting is successful.

> **Follow instructions**

> Put tasks in the order in which they need to be completed

> Make sure tasks are completed on time

Activity: Planning a meeting

Imagine you are holding a meeting to discuss this unit of work with your class group. For the meeting you must create a plan, as well as an agenda, and any other accompanying documents.

Check

- Always make sure that you know how many people are attending the meeting. This will help you plan all the other arrangements.

- Always follow a logical sequence when planning a meeting so you do not forget any important details.

L03 Support a meeting

Your work in supporting a meeting could affect whether or not it is likely to be a success. As a host you will have to carry out a number of administration tasks including welcoming delegates and serving refreshments. Other tasks you may need to carry out are shown in the diagram opposite.

Taking notes

Taking notes at a meeting is an essential task and it is important that the notes follow a logical sequence. The normal way of taking notes is to have a piece of paper which includes the agenda items as headings, with space to write in between the headings. Using this method helps the notes tie up with what has been said at the meeting.

The notes should be laid out in such a way that there is space both to record any decisions that have been taken and to show who is to carry out any actions. This is important. Often meetings can take a long time and people may forget what they have agreed to do unless it has been noted down.

Case study:
Sprite & Co

It soon becomes clear that the meetings arranged at Sprite & Co are not going as well as planned. The company was expecting to win the NHS contracts quite easily – after all Sprite & Co is a leading supplier which has supplied the NHS for a number of years – but this is not happening.

Something is not right so, in an attempt to find out what the problem is, Jane Tapp has decided to review the way meetings are planned. It quickly becomes clear what the problems are:

1. The rooms being used to host the meetings have no natural light and are quite dismal. On average the contract meetings last between three and four hours and this is a long time to sit in miserable surroundings.

2. The meeting rooms are not tidied between meetings and empty cups and half eaten biscuits are left lying around.

3. It seems that visitors are left waiting in the reception area for a long time before meetings take place.

Activity: Group discussion

Why do you think all the factors in the case study might affect the decision making process in the contract meetings?

What can be done in the future to improve the situation?

| Taking simple notes | Signing delegates in and issuing name badges |

Other tasks undertaken to support meeting

| Recording non-attendance | Recording attendance |

Activity: More documents!

This activity follows on from the activity on page 107: Planning a meeting.

You have now arranged your meeting and the last thing you need to do is organise name badges and attendance documentation. Create a name badge for each delegate attending your meeting and a register that can be used for recording attendance and non-attendance.

Check

- Supporting a meeting means providing administrative support to make sure it runs smoothly.

L04 Complete follow-up activities after a meeting

It is very important when a meeting draws to an end that a number of essential tasks are completed. These tasks range from making sure that the meeting room is tidied up to making sure that documents are distributed after the meeting to relevant colleagues. The table below includes some of the key follow-up activities that must be undertaken after a meeting has finished.

Follow-up activity	Why that activity is important
Clearing the room for the next meeting	It is important to carry out this task so that there is no hold-up between meetings. It would be very unprofessional to keep colleagues waiting while a room is being tidied.
Helping colleagues	Provide support to colleagues. For example, give directions to where they want to go if they do not work at your company. Other support would include practical things such as helping a colleague carry paperwork and equipment back to an office.
Understanding the need for privacy	Very often senior managers have private matters to discuss after the meeting has finished. It is therefore important to respect this by not moving in and out of a room where they are discussing private matters.
Tidying up	Tidying up is very important and this includes both confidential and non-confidential information. Confidential information may need to be securely taken to a specific place or possibly shredded after the meeting.
Have notes checked for accuracy	Any notes taken in the meeting must be accurate. It is always wise to get a colleague who attended the meeting with you to check that what you have written is accurate.
Distribution of documents	You may need to send documents such as minutes, presentation slides and other paperwork to colleagues at a later date. This must be done promptly and all data must be accurate and understandable.

Activity: Follow-up tasks

For this task you need to contact the Administration Manager at your centre and ask if you can help to undertake some of the follow-up activities after a meeting has taken place.

Activity: Preparing minutes

Minutes are a record of a meeting. In pairs discuss what they might record.

Look at the Sprite & Co minutes of a meeting on page 105. Consider whether this record would be better described as decision notes and write down your ideas. Share your ideas as a group and go on to discuss the following questions:

Who should decide on the format of the minutes?

In what circumstances would you consider recording the discussion that led up to a decision?

Who are the minutes prepared for?

Are the minutes used as a form of communication between those present at the meeting and other staff in the business? If so, what does this say about the best format for them?

Check

- Always make sure that delegates are signed in and out of meetings. This is not only for the benefit of the business that is hosting the meeting but also for fire safety reasons.

- Follow-up activities are as important as the meeting itself. If you promise to do something, make sure that is exactly what you do.

ASSESSMENT OVERVIEW

While working through this unit, you will have prepared for completing the following assessment tasks:

○	1.1	List the requirements for holding a formal meeting	Pages 102–104
○	1.2	Identify the types of documents which support business meetings	Pages 104–105
○	2.1	Present a plan for setting up a room for a meeting	Pages 106–107
○	2.2	Set up a room for a meeting	Pages 106–107
○	3.1	Provide support at a meeting	Pages 108–109
○	3.2	Take notes at a meeting showing the key action points agreed	Page 108
○	4.1	Clear a room after a meeting	Pages 110–111
○	4.2	Complete follow-up activities after a meeting	Pages 110–111

edexcel

Assignment tips

- You might find it useful to create a table listing the different types of business documents used to support business meetings, and then identify what they do. This will help you establish what you are trying to achieve with each document when you come to set up a meeting.

- When you take notes at a meeting make a list of who was present and whether anyone sent their apologies for being unable to attend. Keep a list of action points identified at the meeting. Remember to list who needs to do what by when, as these are really important bits of information that people will need.

- You need to produce all the documents that attendees would expect to receive after a meeting. You may not need to send these to the attendees, but you will need to submit them to your tutor.

BUSINESS ADMINISTRATION GROUP PROJECT

When working as an administrator in business you will often need to work with other people. In many situations, a group of people can be more productive than one person working on their own. Throughout this unit you will get the chance to develop many key skills including communication, working as a team member, self-management and problem solving.

In this unit you will:

- Find out about an aspect of local business administration
- Demonstrate work-related skills in presenting information as a team member
- Assess own work-related skills in finding out about an aspect of business administration

Why do you think businesses want people to work together well?

L01 Explore an aspect of local business administration

The job of an administrator is varied. This means that people working in the role must be flexible and willing to take on many different roles and tasks. As a result, working in administration can be worthwhile and rewarding.

Below are some of the tasks you may need to complete when working as an administrator:

- Supporting a meeting
- Working on reception
- Dealing with communications including letters, emails, telephone calls and SMS messages
- Organising security
- Dealing with health and safety issues
- Managing recycling and other environmental procedures (for example, minimising waste)
- Dealing with administration systems, i.e. entering data into a computer or creating reports
- Communicating with staff from different parts of the organisational structure.

For more details about the different tasks you might be involved with, see *Unit 14 Working in business and administration*, pages 18–19.

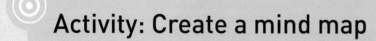

Activity: Create a mind map

Create a mind map of the eight administrative tasks listed above. On your mind map show all the activities you can think of that are involved for each task. For example, show what an administrator would have to do in order to support a meeting.

Aspects of business administration

To complete this unit you will need to make contact with a business and discuss the role of business administration within the organisation. A visit to the business would provide you with the best research opportunities, although you could also contact the company by telephone.

Whichever method you choose to make contact, it is important you research the administrative roles above.

Activity: Group task

Functional skills

You will be practising your **English** and **ICT** skills by researching different businesses.

1. In small groups, and using the list on page 114, choose five aspects of business administration that you would like to learn more about. In discussion with your tutor, select one of your five choices to explore further.

2. You should now carry out some research to find a suitable company for your task. A suitable company is one that often uses this aspect of business administration. Use the Internet, local newspapers or a telephone directory to identify different businesses that could help you with your research.

3. As a group you need to decide what tasks should be completed for your research. You then need to decide who is doing what. Prepare an action plan, so that everyone in your group is clear about what they need to do. An example of an action plan is given below.

4. After carrying out your research into different businesses, you might find it useful to read through the guidance for using different communication technologies (see *Unit 15 Communicating electronically*, page 33).

Business Administration Group Project Action Plan			
Name of Company: XYZ Industries			
Action	To be carried out by who	Date to be completed by	Outcome
Draw up questionnaire	Andy	27/9/2010	To have drawn up a questionnaire
Telephone company	James	28/9/2010	Obtain a name of contact
Internet research	Sabia	28/9/2010	Find out more about business
Write up questions to ask at visit	Mandy	29/9/2010	Know who is asking what when visiting company

Check

- Carry out research into one administrative aspect of a business.

- Choose which aspect of business administration to focus on by looking at the list on page 114.

L01 Teamwork

To complete this unit successfully, you must work as part of a team. It is important to develop team working skills as most employers will expect you to be able to work with your colleagues with little or no support.

Team working is an essential skill to learn. It is very difficult for one person to attempt a large project or task by themselves. It is much easier to break the task down and get team members to take responsibility for an aspect of work and complete it. Working as a team means you can produce lots of ideas. This can be useful when trying to solve a problem.

The mind map below shows six ways in which you can be more effective as a team member:

＊ Key term

Responsibility
When you are responsible for a task, it is your duty to complete the task on time and follow any instructions you have been given.

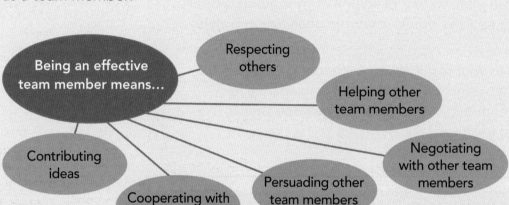

Being an effective team member means...
- Respecting others
- Helping other team members
- Negotiating with other team members
- Persuading other team members
- Cooperating with other members
- Contributing ideas

Activity: Team working

Work in pairs or small groups to build a bridge which spans a metre gap and can carry the weight of a small object. The bridge must be no lower than 30 cm from the floor. You are to make the bridge out of everyday materials (for example, newspaper, sticky tape, paper clips, etc.). The winning team is the one which constructs the bridge that holds the most weight and looks the best.

Sources of information

When carrying out the research for this unit it is important to use both primary and secondary research.

Primary research is the type that you carry out yourself, for example by drawing up a questionnaire or interviewing a member of staff on a visit to a company. Primary research is also known as field or original research.

Secondary research is information you get from other sources (it is not research you have carried out yourself). For example, reading an article on the Internet or in a newspaper is secondary research.

In general terms, primary research is often thought to be more reliable and accurate than secondary research.

Primary research
Original research carried out by you, for example a questionnaire.

Secondary research
Research carried out by another person which you have used in your work, for example a quotation from a book.

Activity: Research task

Working on your own, you are going to research four theorists who specialise in motivation. Use textbooks and the Internet to prepare a short presentation for your group.

The theorists you need to research are:

- Elton Mayo
- Frederick Herzberg
- Douglas McGregor
- Frederick Winslow Taylor

Check

- You will need to understand the benefits of teamwork to an individual and a business.

- You will need to complete primary and secondary research for the group project.

L01 The Internet

The Internet is a fantastic source of information which has made the process of information gathering far easier than it was ten years ago. However, as with most readily available resources, it must be used with some caution. Due to the 'open' nature of the Internet, it is very easy for people to 'post' information on websites, and sometimes it is not necessarily 100 per cent correct. For this reason you must not rely solely upon the Internet – instead, use the Internet and compare it to another reliable source.

Internet search engines

The Internet is a massive database of information and for this reason it can be impossible to find quickly the piece of information that you are looking for. 'Search engines' help you search for information.

A search engine, in simple terms, searches for information that matches what you have written in the text input screen. You may notice on occasions that you search for one thing and something completely unrelated is found. If this happens, you may need to change the text you are searching for to get a better match.

Activity: Using Internet search engines

First of all, choose a partner. Then, on your own, write down 15 questions that you think your partner will not know the answer to. Your partner will do the same for you.

Swap questions. Individually you are to research the answers to the questions on the Internet and then come together as a pair to check that your answers are correct.

Confidentiality

It is important to keep data confidential, and simple steps need to be taken, for example locking drawers and filing cabinets. If data gets into the wrong hands it could be potentially damaging in a personal sense to the general public. It could also be commercially damaging to a business if the information gets into the hands of a competitor.

You need to be careful with the information you gather in your research. The businesses you talk to might tell you sensitive information that they would not want everyone to know.

If information that is confidential 'gets out' and becomes public, it is known as leaked data.

 **Key term**

Leaked data
Information that is made available to the public when a business or individual wants to keep the information to themselves.

Activity: Leaked data

Use the Internet to research one incident of data being leaked to the general public. Over the last few years there have been several high profile cases.

Report back to your tutor using a presentation to explain what you have found and what it might have meant for the person that the leaked data related to.

Check

- It is your responsibility as a data user to make sure that you follow the Data Protection Act at all times, otherwise you may be personally liable for any problems caused.

- Remember that confidentiality applies to written information as well as digital data.

L02 Work-related skills

Communication skills

A key skill that you will need to develop throughout this piece of research is communication. It is very important that when you are communicating with a person, a group or an organisation, you clearly get across what you need to say. Communication comes in many forms including spoken, written or visual (for example, diagrams). Whichever method is being used it must be suitable and clear.

Communication methods	Advantages	Disadvantages
Written	Permanent record Easy to understand Can be confidential	Takes time to prepare Can be confusing if poorly written
Spoken	Instant feedback Quick Cheap	'Chinese whisper' effect can distort the message Can be misunderstood easily if not clearly presented
Visual	Difficult concepts can be easily demonstrated May appeal to some people more than written or spoken methods	Usually needs to be accompanied by a written or spoken explanation leading to more work Can be expensive if high-quality colour images are being used

Activity: Contacting the business you are researching

In your group, write a letter to the organisation you are researching. You need to tell the organisation about your BTEC Entry 3/Level 1 Business Administration course, what you would like its help with, and include your contact details for it to reply.

It is important that your letter is professionally written and accurate. You might want to check the guidance given in *Unit 19 Creating business documents*, page 87–89.

Listening and questioning skills

To make your research effective you need to develop good listening and questioning skills. There are certain things you can do to make sure that you actively listen and ask questions:

- If possible, make eye contact with the person who is speaking

- Make notes of what is being said

- Do not interrupt

- Ask **open questions**

- Do not be critical or negative.

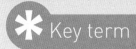
Open questions

Open questions require a longer answer than 'yes' or 'no'.

'What kind of meetings do you organise?' is an open question. Compare that to 'Do you organise scheduled meetings?'

Think about how an interviewee's answer might be different for each question. How much information are you likely to get from their answer?

Team member

Working effectively as part of a team is important for your future career. There are ways that you can improve your personal effectiveness as a team member. Look back to the mind map on page 116 which shows how you can make an effective contribution as a team member.

Activity: Practice interview

Working as a group, assume you have arranged a visit to interview an employee at the business you are researching. Role play typical questions (including open ones) and scenarios you may come across on your visit, so that you are confident when carrying out the interview. For example, you could ask a question like: 'In what ways do you feel you contribute to the team you work in?'

Check

- When contacting businesses, it is important that your message is clear and easy to understand.

- Being an effective team member is important for your future career, and for this unit.

L02 Self-management

Self-management is the skill of being able to complete tasks on time through good time management. Effective self-management means that you will be a more effective team member.

Good self-managers will understand their limitations in terms of how much work they can complete in a given amount of time. Also, good self-managers are flexible – they can change their plans quickly to take on board new ideas or suggestions.

When working on the research project, there will be times when you will have to work as a self-manager to complete the tasks you have been set. The table below shows the key requirements of a good self-manager.

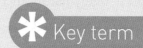

Key term

Self-management
The process of organising your time and your work in order to successfully complete tasks.

Prioritising

When you are managing a number of different tasks, you may need to prioritise your work. This is when you decide which task is most urgent. Sometimes the easiest way to set priorities is by working out when each task needs to be completed by – the one that needs to be completed soonest is your top priority.

Self-management skill	Why is this skill important?
Flexibility	This is an important skill because, for this project, you may have to change your original plans and ideas. On a wider scale, employers need employees that are flexible and willing to change, otherwise they will get left behind as technology and procedures move on.
Organising self	It is impossible to be a successful self-manager if you cannot organise yourself. Organising yourself involves getting all the materials together that you need for your job and making sure you know what is expected of you.
Accepting responsibility	Accepting responsibility is important because colleagues need to know that they can trust you to get things done. After all, their job might depend on you doing something first. It is also important to accept responsibility if you make a mistake, otherwise someone else may be blamed unfairly. This will also damage trust within your team and affect the way the team works.
Completing all tasks set and on time	It is important that you complete all the tasks you have agreed to do so that the team is not held up. Also, on many occasions in business, tasks have to be completed by a certain time otherwise this could cause problems and delays. It is also important that you complete all tasks for this piece of research work as your fellow team members will be relying on you to do so.

! Remember

- If you are flexible and change your plans to fit in with other people, there may come a time when they can do the same for you.

Activity: Prioritising your work

This task requires you to work individually. Imagine that you work in an office. Below are a range of everyday tasks that you must complete. Place them in order of priority giving reasons for your choice:

- Support a meeting to discuss an event tomorrow evening

- Deal with communications including letters, emails, telephone calls and SMS messages from attenders and non-attenders at the event tomorrow evening

- Organise security for an event tomorrow evening

- Deal with health and safety issues relating to an event tomorrow evening

- Deal with administration systems – for example, entering data or creating reports – this is part of your normal daily routine

- Liaise with staff from different parts of the organisation to make sure everyone is informed about tomorrow evening's event.

✔ Check

- To complete this unit successfully, you will need to manage your work effectively.

L02 Problem solving

A key skill in being an effective group worker is the ability to solve problems. Often when carrying out research things do not go to plan. There are many types of problems, some of which are small and others that are slightly larger.

However, one of the most important skills you can have is the ability to overcome problems. The diagram below shows some of the potential problems you could face while working as an administrator.

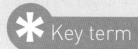
✳ Key term

Problem solving
The process of developing creative and flexible solutions to problems that may arise.

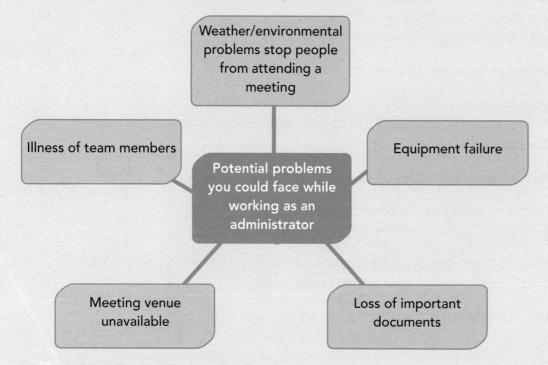

Some of these problems could be avoided through planning. For example, book a venue for a meeting well in advance of the date of the meeting. If you leave it too late, you might find that the venue you want will not be available.

However, some problems such as weather or illness may be unavoidable. It is best to think about and plan what could be done to reduce the effect these things may have on your plans.

◎ Activity: Problems

In your group make a list of the problems you might face while carrying out this piece of research. Suggest at least one way you could get round each problem.

Presentation skills

When you are giving a presentation, you should consider the following guidelines:

- Try to keep the amount of text on a slide to a minimum – the slides should support what you are saying rather than be a script

- If you have handouts, make sure you have enough copies for all the attendees

- Remember to leave time for any questions at the end of the presentation

- Make sure you have all the equipment you need for the presentation, including a venue

- Speak slowly and clearly.

Activity: Present your findings

As a group, you will need to present the findings of your research back to your tutor and the rest of the group. In order to do this, each member of the group will need to contribute to the planning and the presentation.

Check

- Planning can help you to solve problems before they happen.

- Some problems cannot be avoided, but there are usually things you can do to reduce their effect.

- You need to plan your work as a team in order to make the most of your presentation.

L03 Assess own work

The process of receiving **feedback** and setting **targets** helps you to improve your skills. When you receive feedback from your tutor, your work will improve if you are able to take their comments on board. In the workplace you will receive feedback from your manager, and if you take in their comments, your work will improve and so will your chances of promotion and better pay.

In order to complete this unit, you need to receive feedback and set targets for improvement. Feedback may come from your tutor or from your peers (that is, other learners on your course).

Providing feedback

If you are going to give feedback on someone's performance, you need to remember that people can be sensitive. While feedback should be honest, it should always be constructive (that is, helpful). If you feel that someone needs to improve something, you could try:

- Identifying something that they did really well, and then

- Identifying the area you think they need to improve, giving examples and suggestions if you can.

For example:

Feedback:

I thought your contribution to the team was really good - you were enthusiastic and came up with some very good ideas. If you were to look for an area for improvement, I think it would be your time management. There were a couple of times when you didn't meet a deadline, which meant someone else wasn't able to start work when they thought they needed to.

Activity: How good is your work?

When you have completed your research, your tutor will assess what you have done. After you have made any changes it would be a good idea to send a copy to the business you have researched. They will be pleased that you have shown an interest in the business and they might even use some of your suggestions.

After you have shown the business your work, ask them if they will provide feedback on it.

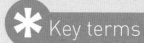
Key terms

Feedback
Constructive and helpful comments that will help you to identify what you have done well and what you can improve.

Targets
Things you want to achieve, also known as objectives. These are usually goals you want to complete in the next 6 or 12 months in order to improve your performance at work.

Setting targets

Once you have received some feedback, think about how you will address any issues that have been raised. First, you should write down your strengths and areas for improvement. You might want to draw up a table like the one below.

Strengths	Areas for improvement
Enthusiastic	Time management
Came up with some good ideas	

Now work out how you can improve the areas identified. For example, if you need to improve your time management skills, you could keep a diary of all the tasks you have to complete. This will help you manage your priorities and keep track of when you have a deadline coming up.

Targets should be reviewed regularly to make sure you are working towards them effectively. The best way to judge a target is to make it as specific as possible. For example, a target of 'improve my time keeping' is not very helpful as it is impossible to measure.

Try to set dates and include quantities, to make sure your targets are measurable. So, for example, the target could be 'to submit all my coursework on or before the deadline for the rest of the year'.

Activity: Setting targets

With your tutor, agree on what targets you will set, and how you will measure them. You will need to review your progress towards these targets regularly, so make sure you keep them safe.

Check

- It is important that feedback is constructive – this has to be something that someone can work with.

- Targets should be measurable and practical in order to be effective.

ASSESSMENT OVERVIEW

While working through this unit, you will have prepared for completing the following assessment tasks:

edexcel

Assignment tips

- As a team, one of your first tasks should be to work out what tasks need to be completed as part of the group project. This will help give roles for different team members and prevent anyone doing the same tasks as someone else. It will also avoid anything being forgotten.

- When you receive feedback, remember that no one is perfect. There are always things that people can do to improve their work, and some things will be harder work and take longer than other things. Be realistic about what you expect from yourself and make sure your targets are practical and manageable.

IDEAS FOR SMALL BUSINESSES

By completing this course you will have developed a good level of skill in many business areas. This unit gives you the chance to apply what you have learned by developing your own business idea. You will learn important business skills, including how to carry out market research and you will look into production and selling costs. At the end of the unit you will bring together all that you have learned by producing a business plan.

In this unit you will:

- Be able to select an idea for a small business using work-based skills

- Be able to carry out market research for your small business idea

- Be able to produce a simple business plan

Have you got the right skills to be successful in business?

L01 Select an idea for a business

Business ideas

Some of the most successful business people in the world started out by coming up with a simple business idea. Very often the simplest ideas are the best. This is because customers can understand them easily and they are simple to bring into reality.

Over the last 100 years, industry has changed. Fifty years ago the manufacturing sector (businesses that focus on producing a product) made up the largest part of the UK's economy.

However, more recently industries such as banking and insurance (sometimes called the service sector) now create more wealth for the UK than factories. Therefore, when you are considering possible ideas, try to think about services you could offer as well as products you could sell.

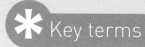

Key terms

Manufacturing sector
This includes businesses that focus on making a product.

Service sector
The service sector includes industries that provide a service such as banking and insurance.

Customer needs
The needs of customers that a business must consider when developing a product.

Activity: Business pioneers

Use the Internet to find out who are the top ten most successful business people in the world.

Create a table that includes their name, the name of their business and what their business does.

Customer needs

A business can only survive if there is demand for its products or services. Over the years there have been many companies and people spending large amounts of money on developing products only to find later that very few people want to buy them.

Nowadays, businesses spend a lot of money and time researching the market to check that a market exists for their products when they are launched. However, there are no guarantees and even the biggest companies have launched products that have been unsuccessful.

Activity: Success or flop

Below is an example of a bad invention.

Individually, use the Internet to carry out research to find five successful products and five products that have been unsuccessful.

While carrying out your research, try to identify which company was behind each product.

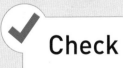

Check

- A business idea will only be successful if customers want what the company is making. This is known as meeting customer needs.

- Businesses carry out extensive market research before launching a product. This way they have a better chance of making sure that the item meets the customers' needs.

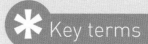

L01 Costs

Production costs

Many products have been launched and have been successful. However, in the long run, the costs of production have far outweighed the selling costs. The luxury car market is a good example. If a manufacturer cannot sell enough luxury cars to cover the costs of production, then the production and selling of the cars must stop. If not, the business could end up losing a lot of money.

It is important that you think very carefully about how much an item will cost to make and sell when you are considering the product or service you are going to launch.

Selling costs

Selling costs can be the forgotten cost in business. Often a person or business will launch a potentially successful idea but will forget to think about the costs of selling that item. Each of these individual costs can be quite small. However, there are often a lot of them and, when put together, they can mount up. If cash has not been set aside, a good idea can fail through poor planning and a lack of cash flow.

Examples of selling costs include:

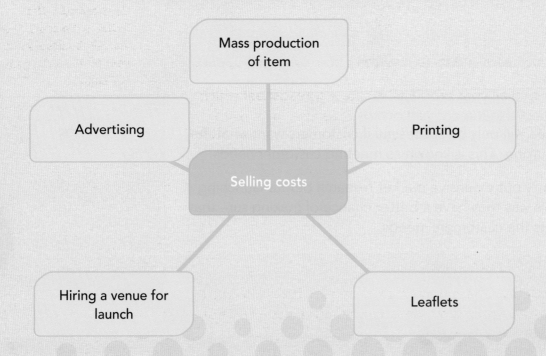

Activity: Different types of cost

1. Individually, create a presentation that explains:

- production costs

- selling costs

- fixed costs

- variable costs

- start-up costs

- running costs.

Use the Internet to help with your research.

2. You need to provide three examples of each type of cost.

3. Now try to work out which costs would be most relevant to your business idea. Give an explanation of this in your presentation.

Activity: What is the cost?

As a group you are going to start up a small social enterprise company that makes biscuits and muffins. You then have to sell the products you have made. During the production process keep a close eye on your costs and make a note of how much you spend.

After you have sold all your products, create a spreadsheet which allows you to work out the production costs, selling costs, fixed costs, variable costs, start-up costs and running costs. You will need help from your tutor to complete this task successfully.

Functional skills

By completing the 'What is the cost?' task you will be developing your Mathematics and ICT skills.

Check

- A business can only survive if the money coming in from the sale of its goods and services is greater than the production costs of those goods.

L01 Research and sources of information

Businesses carry out research using a lot of different sources. Companies exist whose only purpose is to carry out research on behalf of other businesses. This can be expensive!

You will not need to carry out research that is as in-depth as that produced by a market research business. However, you must do some research to make sure your idea is feasible (that is, that there is likely to be a market for it). The table below gives some ideas about where you can find market research information.

Research source	What will the source tell me?
Internet	Contains information on almost any product that is available on the market. The Internet also has many review sites where users can provide feedback on products and ideas. If you wish to pay, you can also get current in-depth market research data from market research businesses.
Newspapers	Provide information on new companies opening up or businesses closing down. This will give you an idea of the levels of competition and demand. Newspapers also contain lots of advertising so you can get an idea of how others are trying to sell their products.
Business directory, e.g. Yellow Pages	Provides contact details of businesses selling the same or similar products or services to your idea. Again, you can assess the competition.

Research source	What will the source tell me?
Magazines 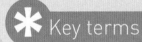	Provide information on competitors, often in the form of product reviews. Magazines also include glossy pictures which show you what competitor products look like.
Market research reports	These reports are available online (although very expensive) or at any major local library. They are very detailed and contain lots of facts and figures about the state of a specific market and how well different products are selling. These documents would be one of the most useful sources of information for a major business.

Activity: Which are the most useful research resources?

For this task you are to work individually.

Carry out a small piece of research to find out which are the top ten selling cars of the year. Use as many of the sources from the table as you can to do this.

Write down which were the most helpful sources and explain why.

Check

- 'Sources of information' relates to where information can be found to help solve a problem or provide research to support your work.

- Research is only of any use if it is reliable and accurate.

L01 Communication and other skills

Good communication skills are vital in business. This is particularly true when you are trying to gain interest in, or sell, your product. It is important that you speak clearly when you are discussing your idea so that people can get a good idea of what you are describing.

Again, as mentioned earlier in this book, you must apply good listening skills. You need to appear professional when dealing with important people. The same is true for written communication. It must be accurate in every way including spelling, punctuation, layout and choice of images, and so on.

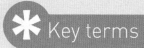

Activity: Sales presentation

For this task you are to work individually.

Imagine you work in sales and must choose a product you would like to sell. Prepare a convincing sales presentation for the item you have chosen and deliver it to your tutor or group.

Team member

As mentioned in *Unit 22 Business administration group project* (starting on page 113), it is important to work as part of a team so that jobs can be completed in less time. Working as a team is also vital if a problem crops up – many people can make suggestions to try to solve it.

Self-management

As mentioned in *Unit 22*, self-management is a large part of the success of any business venture. As a team member, you must be reliable so that others can trust you to carry out the tasks that you have agreed to do. Being a good self-manager means that you must be flexible and willing to work with new ideas or suggestions.

Problem solving

As mentioned in *Unit 22*, good business people tend to be skilled at solving problems. It is unlikely that everything will go to plan. There are often parts of a plan that you might not have thought about, or something might have changed. If this happens you must be open to suggestions and flexible when solving the problems that may crop up.

Activity: Personal skills

Think of times in your life when you have had to:

- be part of a team

- be a self-manager

- solve problems.

Create a collage with images that represent these three situations.

For each situation, write brief notes to explain how you handled it.

Check

- Communication skills are essential skills to make sure that spoken, written and visual messages are clearly transmitted and received.

- Self-management is the process of managing your time so that you can successfully complete all tasks to a deadline.

L02 Market research techniques and L03 producing a simple business plan

The table on pages 134–135 provides some suggestions of published or secondary sources of information. However, in business, information is no good if it is out of date. Therefore, companies often carry out primary market research. They do this in many different ways including:

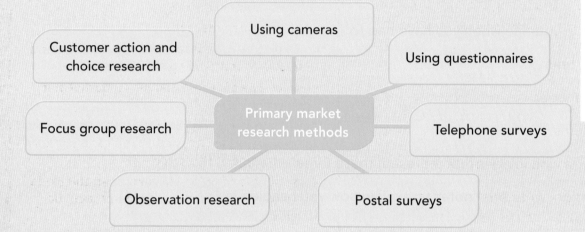

- Using cameras
- Customer action and choice research
- Using questionnaires
- Focus group research
- Primary market research methods
- Telephone surveys
- Observation research
- Postal surveys

Activity: Benefits and drawbacks of research methods

In pairs, research the benefits and drawbacks of each of the methods highlighted above. Put your findings into a briefing paper which will be given to all other group members.

Activity: Research task for business idea

On your own, carry out some market research to work out how successful your business idea might be. Use at least three different research methods (including primary and secondary) so that you can build a more complete picture of your market.

Refer to the previous activity above when choosing the most suitable research methods.

Produce a simple business plan reflecting market research

For any start-up business, the business plan is the most important document that needs to be prepared. The reason for this is that a good business plan may encourage **investors** to take a **risk** and invest in your idea. Importantly, for the business owners, a business plan gives a clear view of what the business is aiming to do in the short, medium and long term. Business plans tend to focus on three main areas:

- An outline of your business idea

- An outline of the market you are trying to launch into

- An outline of your financial structure.

On the right is an example of the information that needs to be included in a business plan.

Business Plan for XYZ Company

- ↳ Outline of business idea
    - o Description of product service
    - o Reason for designing product/ starting business?
    - o Anyone else involved with you in this venture?
- ↳ Outline of the market
    - o Who are you aiming the product or service at?
    - o Competitors?
    - o Customers?
- ↳ An outline of yourself and your background in business including experience
- ↳ An outline of how you intend to market and sell your idea
- ↳ An outline of how you are going to price your product or service, and an indication of how you arrived at this price
- ↳ An outline of technical resources and skills needed to produce or provide product or service.

Activity: Business plan for your idea

For this unit you need to produce a business plan for your business idea. Have a look at the example above or carry out some Internet research into other layouts. Often banks will provide business plan templates on their websites. This might be a good place to look in order to get you started.

Using the headings and information you need to include in a business plan, create your plan using a word-processing program.

 Key terms

Investors
People or businesses that give a business money. They invest in the business because they expect to receive some of the profits.

Investment risk
A risk in business is often based on how likely it is that a business or investors will lose money.

Check

- A product or service idea needs to be researched in depth.

- For a business idea to be successful, it must be designed with a target market in mind.

 Functional skills

By producing a structured document clearly explaining your business idea, you will be practising your **English** skills.

ASSESSMENT OVERVIEW

While working through this unit, you will have prepared for completing the following assessment tasks:

○	1.1	Select a small business idea to research	Pages 130–133
○	1.2	Demonstrate work-based skills by: • Communicating clearly • Working as a team member • Demonstrating self-management skills • Problem solving	Pages 136–137
○	2.1	Plan simple market research	Pages 134–135
○	2.2	Carry out simple market research	Pages 134–135
○	3.1	Produce a simple business plan reflecting the market research	Pages 138–139

edexcel :::

Assignment tips

- You need to show that you have chosen a business idea from a range of possible ideas. Once you have identified a range of different ideas, you might want to write a list of the pros and cons for each idea in order to choose the best one. Keep this list so you can use it for your assessment for this unit.

- When you produce your business plan, you need to include the following information:

  o What the product or service is

  o When and where the product or service is to be sold, and at what price

  o The target market for the product or service

  o The human, physical and financial resources you need to offer the product or service

  o How you plan to pay for the set-up costs

  o How you will advertise and sell the product or service to customers.

JOB OPPORTUNITIES IN BUSINESS ADMINISTRATION

Once you have completed your BTEC course in Business Administration you can start to apply for jobs in administration. Through this unit you will explore job opportunities that are available across different areas of business.

You will also investigate conditions of employment including contracts of employment, qualifications and skills needed for different administration roles. Finally, you will start making plans for your future after you successfully complete this course.

In this unit you will:

- Know about job opportunities in business administration

- Know about terms and conditions of employment within business administration

- Know about the qualifications and skills needed for jobs in administration

- Be able to plan how to start work within business administration

What does your future hold for you?

L01 Job opportunities

Through studying Business Administration and successfully completing this course, a whole new world of job opportunities will open up for you.

It is important to research job opportunities (for example, what the job involves, what the company is like) as understanding the job can help you find something you enjoy and will be successful at. Often people see a job advertised that they like the sound of but they do not really know what the job will involve or the qualifications and skills needed to get that job.

This can cause problems because, if they are constantly being turned down for jobs, it will affect their self-esteem and confidence in applying for other jobs. A little preparation beforehand would make it easier for them to identify jobs for which they are suited and reduce all the stress of being turned down.

Activity: Researching different jobs

Use the Internet to research opportunities within the business administration job sector. Try to find ten jobs and get an idea of what they involve.

After carrying out your research, choose three of the jobs and create realistic job advertisements for them.

To help you, have a look at the diagram below which contains a number of job titles.

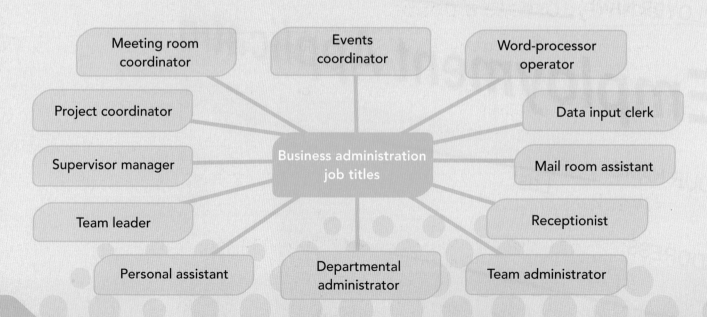

Functional areas

The phrase 'functional area' simply means 'department'. In order to run a large business successfully, it is important to have specialist staff who can deal with the tasks that need to be done.

In smaller businesses you may find that one person does all the tasks or the work is spread among a small number of people. Large businesses are made up of several main functional areas which will usually include:

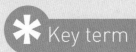

Key term

Functional areas
Different parts or departments of a business that focus on a limited range of important tasks.

Production

Facilities Management

Finance

Research and Development

Functional areas of a business

IT Support

Customer Service

Marketing and Sales

Human Resources

Activity: Research functional areas

Work in pairs and carry out research into functional areas. You need to do this in the following way:

- Choose one functional area and research the job roles that exist within it
- Find out what a company structure chart is
- Research what is meant by 'chain of command' and 'span of control'.

Activity: Create a poster

Create a poster which indicates all the job roles included in the functional area you have investigated.

To make your poster professional you are to draw your job roles on a company structure chart.

Present your poster to the rest of your group.

✓ Check

- It is important to get a full picture of what a job involves and the skills and qualifications needed to fulfil a post before you apply. A little research early on will reduce the frustration later.

L02 Terms and conditions of employment

Work patterns

In today's business world, organisations cannot afford to close for long periods of time between working days.

Many businesses, particularly those involved in the production sector, stay open for 24 hours a day, 7 days a week, 365 days a year. It is therefore important to know the different terms that describe work patterns. The term 'work pattern' simply means the way a person's working hours are organised.

The table below explains a range of typical work patterns you will come across when researching jobs.

✱ Key term

Work pattern
The way a person's working hours are organised, for example times, days of the week.

Work pattern	Explanation
Shift work	When an employee usually works different hours on different weeks. Usually, shift work is used when a business needs to stay open all the time. Examples include factories and 24-hour supermarkets. Normally shift work will follow a two or three week pattern. For example, during the first week, an employee may work 6 a.m. to 2 p.m. and 2 p.m. to 10 p.m. If it is a three shift pattern (sometimes known as a 'continental' style system) they will work the two shifts plus a third shift from 10 p.m. to 6 a.m.
Early starts	An early start shift pattern is one which starts early in the morning, for example, 4 a.m. An example would be a milkman.
Late finishes	A late finish shift pattern usually refers to working hours which finish after 10 p.m. An example would be a doctor working in a hospital.
Night work	Night work, as the title suggests, is when a person works through the night, maybe starting at 10 p.m. and finishing at 6 a.m. An example would be a nurse.
Weekend work	Weekend work is a popular shift pattern for students. Again, as the name suggests, the working hours are throughout a weekend. A person may work one or both weekend days. An example would be a student working in a DIY store.
Bank holiday work	Bank holiday work is work that is undertaken on national bank holiday weekends. Such hours may be part of a person's contract of employment or additional. An example would be a vehicle repair and rescue worker.
Flexitime	Flexitime is a type of work where a person has core hours of work. A person has to attend work between, for example, the hours of 10 a.m. and 3 p.m. A person must work their normal working week (normally 37.5 hours). However, they can make up their hours at whichever time they choose outside the core hours. An example would be an office worker.

Work pattern	Explanation
Irregular work pattern	An irregular work pattern is one which does not follow the same working hours week after week. An example would be a salesman.
Days off during the week	Traditionally shopkeepers used to close for one day a week to make up for working weekends. However, in most businesses this is not the case. A person would take a day off in the week to make sure that they did not work more than their full-time working hours. This might be the case if the job they did involved working weekends. An example would be a full-time shop assistant in a department store.
Annual leave	Annual leave is the time each employee is allowed to take off as holiday. Annual leave for a typical full-time job in the UK is 28 days. However, this can increase depending on how long you have worked for the company.

Activity: Different work patterns

Carry out research into the ten work patterns shown in the table.

Choose one job type for each work pattern (it should be different from the example given in the table).

Put together a presentation for your tutor or group.

Check

- Different types of jobs need employees to work different work patterns. For example, teachers work different hours from nurses.

- If you are asked to work irregular hours you may be paid an extra amount of money on top of your normal hourly rate.

L02 Pay and benefits

Pay

Getting paid is the reason most people work. However, enjoying the job you do and feeling valued are also important factors – especially for your self-esteem.

It is important to know that there are different ways in which people are paid. Nowadays, most employed staff are paid monthly straight into their bank account. In many jobs there are also opportunities to increase your wage by getting promotion or taking on more responsibility. This will usually involve moving up a salary scale. A salary scale is a document which highlights how much people should be paid at different levels in an organisation.

The diagram below provides information about **pay**.

Key term

Pay
The amount of money received in return for working.

Hourly
Paid a set amount for every hour worked.

Example job: Shop Assistant.

Monthly
Paid a set amount on a specific day of the month

Example job: Teacher.

Salary Scales
A document which sets out how much employees are paid taking into account their position in the business.

Example job: Banker.

Increments
A term used to explain by how much a person's wage will increase by if, for example, they have gained promotion.

Activity: How much are people paid?

Research how much people get paid for five different jobs. You could do this by visiting a job centre or by researching job sites on the Internet.

After you have carried out your research, create a poster which shows, for each job:

- the responsibilities
- the pay and benefits.

Benefits

Along with pay, many jobs also provide extra **benefits** to employees. These can come in many forms. The reason a business may decide to give these is simple – to **motivate** the people who work for a business. Benefits can also make people think twice about leaving a company to look for another job if the benefits they receive are particularly good.

Examples of benefits which businesses may offer employees are shown below.

- Gym discounts
- Health insurance
- Pension
- Training/professional development
- Benefits which businesses may offer employees
- Rail season ticket discounts
- Subsidised/free meals
- Uniform/clothing allowance
- Bonus pay for overtime

Activity: Know your perks

Pick one of the terms listed in the diagram above and research what it means for the employee.

Try to find three examples of different businesses that give their employees this benefit.

Now present your findings back to the group.

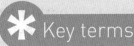

Key terms

Benefits
Extra 'perks' received by employees to encourage loyalty and motivation.

Motivation
Motivation is how much you want to do something. If you are highly motivated, it is likely that you enjoy your job and your work is of a high quality.

✓ Check

- The way in which you are paid may depend on the type of job that you do. For example, some employees are paid an hourly rate while others will be paid an annual salary.

- Often jobs offer other benefits apart from pay. These may include private health care or a company pension.

L03 Qualifications

When you apply for a job, your qualifications and grades are often the first thing a potential employer will look at. In order to present yourself in the best possible way, you need to know:

- What qualifications you have got

- What grades you have achieved

- The type of qualification such as vocational (BTEC, NVQ, etc.) or academic (GCSE).

You also need to know the difference between 'essential' and 'desirable' qualifications. This will help you understand what you need to have in order to apply for a job.

Essential qualifications

Essential qualifications are the ones you need in order to start work in certain jobs or professions. For example, a person cannot work as a qualified accountant until they have passed the relevant professional examinations.

Anyone applying for the job must have these essential qualifications before the business will think about employing them.

Desirable qualifications

Desirable qualifications are different from essential qualifications because you do not necessarily need them to enter a job or profession.

However, employers like job applicants to have other qualifications in addition to essential ones. This shows a wider knowledge and range of skills which the person can offer. For example, this might include qualifications in the skills of word-processing, keyboarding, audio transcription and shorthand.

Practical qualifications

As well as, or instead of, academic or vocational qualifications, employers like job applicants to have practical qualifications. These can include subjects like first aid and lifting and carrying.

As with desirable qualifications, practical qualifications show that the person has a wider range of skills.

Activity: What are my qualifications worth?

Individually, research a range of qualifications which are relevant to business and administration.

You must complete a table like the example below by writing the full name of the qualification, whether the qualification is vocational or academic and the grade value of the qualification.

Try to research at least ten different qualifications. Your tutor will be able to help you with this task.

Full name of qualification	Academic/Vocational	Grade value
E.g. NVQ Business and Administration	Vocational	Level 1

Check

- It is important to understand fully the type and value of a course you are studying.

- Courses vary a lot so it is important you choose the correct one from the outset.

L03 Skills and qualities

When you apply for a job, as well as looking at your qualifications, a potential employer will look at the skills and qualities you will bring to the organisation. Employers look at skills and qualities for three main reasons:

1. To see if you have the skills to do the job you have applied for.

2. To make sure your skills fit in with the business's needs and that no crossover of skills exists with current employees.

3. Employers will want to get an idea of how you will fit into the business as a team member and make sure that you would work well with their other employees.

An employer is likely to look for:

*   Personal qualities including:

    o   Ability to organise yourself

    o   Ability to work well with others

*   Work-related skills including:

    o   Self-organisation

    o   Team working

    o   Problem solving

    o   Self-management

*   A level of fitness that means:

    o   Ability to carry out tasks

    o   Good attendance at work.

Planning

You should now be in a position to start planning to find a job.

However, an important question you must ask yourself is 'What can I offer an employer?' It can be difficult to think of what you have to offer off the top of your head. That is why it is best to use a 'skills scan'. A skills scan is simply a way of assessing your own skills, qualities and qualifications.

Activity: My skills scan

This is an individual task. You need to be totally honest about yourself.

The list below provides the questions you need to ask yourself when checking your skills, along with some sample ideas for responses. It is important that you answer honestly or the whole process will not work.

You need to put your own answers to the questions into a table using a professional looking format.

My skills scan

- **What personal qualities do I possess?**
  - ○ Self-organiser
  - ○ Good communicator
  - ○ Work well with others

- **What work-related skills do I possess?**
  - ○ Good communicator
  - ○ Teamwork
  - ○ Problem solving
  - ○ Good level of fitness to work

- **What skills and abilities do I possess?**
  - ○ Good with ICT
  - ○ Good at maths
  - ○ Deal well with complex problems
  - ○ Good at working under pressure

- **What interests do I have?**
  - ○ Sport
  - ○ Music
  - ○ Nature
  - ○ Cooking

- **What are my values?**
  - ○ Hardworking
  - ○ Honesty

- **What are my personal qualities?**
  - ○ Supportive
  - ○ Caring
  - ○ Can easily adapt to new situations

- **Lifestyle constraints**
  - ○ Want to work in home town
  - ○ Only want to work part-time so I can attend college

Check

- To improve your chance of success when entering the job market, it is important that you plan what you are doing. This will help you know the skills and qualifications needed to be successful in your chosen career.

- It is important to make plans so that you know what you need to do to move to the next stage of your educational or working career.

L04 Finding out about jobs

It is important that you know about different jobs, and routes into jobs, as the employment market is more competitive than ever. Nowadays it is expected that the average person will have between 5 and 15 jobs in a working lifetime.

Many jobs these days ask for experience and this can be difficult if you are looking for a first job. The problem is you cannot get experience because you cannot get a job.

Don't worry – these days many people volunteer in order to get experience. Internships are also becoming more common in the UK. An internship is unpaid employment offered by an organisation. When thinking about these options you must always take a long-term view and remember that a short period of unpaid work could lead to a satisfying lifelong career.

Below are some practical examples of where you can get guidance and help.

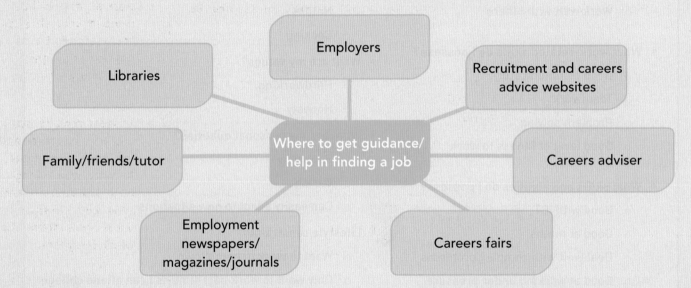

Goals

Before starting to look for a job, you must plan out what you are going to do. The key to planning is to have SMART targets which allow you to focus on what you have to do and by when.

Specific	Goals should be well defined and clear
Measurable	There must be a way of measuring whether a goal has been completed or how far away it is from completion
Achievable	The goal must be attainable (it must be possible to reach the goal)
Realistic	The goal must be something that can be achieved with the available resources, knowledge and time
Timed	There needs to be enough time to complete the goal and there should be a time frame for when the goal should be completed

Activity: Making plans

Create an action plan like the one below. An example of how it needs to be completed is given.

Your action plan should clearly show your short, medium and long term goals. You should also include the steps you have to take to achieve them and a timescale.

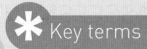 **Key terms**

Short term goals
Those which typically take up to 12 months to achieve. An example of a short term goal would be to achieve a qualification which will allow you to access a particular job or course of study.

Medium term goals
Those which typically take between one and three years to complete. An example of a medium term goal would be to gain work experience in a company that will allow you to get a full-time position or a higher level course of study.

Long term goals
Those which typically take between three and five years to complete. An example of a long term goal could include an ambition to work in a management position within five years.

Action Plan		
Name:	**Date:**	
Steps I need to take?	**By when?**	**How will I know I have been successful?**
	Short term targets:	
E.g. Pass BTEC Course	July 2011	Written confirmation that I have passed the course
	Medium term targets:	
	Long term targets:	

Check

- Different types of jobs will be advertised in different places. When searching for a job remember to look at a range of sources.

- It is important to set goals for yourself so that you have something to aim for. Goals give you direction and help you to achieve your ambitions.

ASSESSMENT OVERVIEW

While working through this unit, you will have prepared for completing the following assessment tasks:

○	1.1	Identify jobs in different sectors of business administration	Page 142
○	1.2	Describe the job roles in one functional area of business administration	Page 143
○	2.1	Describe the terms and conditions of employment within business administration	Pages 144–147
○	3.1	Present information about the qualifications and skills required for selected jobs in business administration	Pages 148–151
○	4.1	Produce a plan to start work within business administration	Pages 152–153

Assignment tips

- You need to identify three different jobs within business administration. You need to give details about the skills, qualities and qualifications required to work in *each* different job role. Since jobs adverts will also include the terms and conditions of the employment, you should also explain what the terms and conditions for each job mean.

- Your career plan should identify one long-term goal and two short-term goals. You should think of short term as within the next 12 to 18 months. A long-term goal could be anything beyond 18 months.

Key terms

Abbreviate – To make a word shorter, either by taking out letters (e.g. 'tomorrow' becomes 'tmro') or by cutting the word short (e.g. 'Saturday' becomes 'Sat').

Accurate – Free from errors. To make sure documents are accurate, you need to check them carefully.

Acronym – Shortening a long name by using the initial letters of each word. For example, the BBC is an acronym for the British Broadcasting Corporation.

Agenda – An agenda is a document that is sent to attendees before a meeting to let them know what is going to be discussed.

Benefits – Extra 'perks' received by employees to encourage loyalty and motivation.

Business documents – Documents either in paper or electronic form which are used in business for a number of different purposes. For the document to be useful, it must be completed with accuracy.

Business goal – A business goal is what the business is aiming to do – this might be as simple as make a profit.

Cash flow – Money flowing in and out of a business in the form of payments and receipts.

Collate – To mix copies of different documents together to give information in a specific order.

Colleague – Someone from the same organisation as you. They could be more junior than you, someone at the same level as you (sometimes called a 'peer'), or someone at a more senior level than you.

Communication skills – The ability to talk and listen to others with a high degree of accuracy.

Comply – To act by the guidelines or rules set out in a law, such as the Data Protection Act. It is a business's legal duty to comply with these laws.

Confidential – Information that should not be shared, such as salary details, company strategies, customer contact details, etc.

Confirm – To check that something is right. For example, if you have missed anything, your tutor should be able to tell you what else you need to do.

Consistent – If something is consistent, it remains the same or largely unchanged.

Correspondence – A broad term for any form of written communication. This could include letters, emails, faxes, text messages, etc.

Customer – Someone to whom you provide a service. This might be someone from a different organisation, or it could be someone who works for the same business as you.

Customer needs – The needs of customers that a business must consider when developing a product.

Cybercrime – A type of crime that uses computers. This can include identity theft, stealing from online bank accounts, stealing information, etc. You have to be very careful with information you give away online to avoid cybercrime.

Data Protection Act – A law which protects the general public from having their personal data misused.

Dealing with mail – A very important operation within a business as many customers still use mail as a way of doing business. Efficient mail delivery ensures that mail does not go missing and customers receive good levels of customer service.

Delegate – Someone attending a meeting. This person may represent another business, and so will want to give a positive impression of their organisation.

Delegate pack – Information given to delegates which is designed to support the meeting.

Email etiquette – Good practice guidelines. These are things to consider when sending emails, and can help avoid embarrassing cases of misunderstanding.

Etiquette – Good manners and thinking about other people. It is good etiquette to refill the photocopier because it would be irritating to have to fill it with paper before you wanted to use it each time.

Feasible – Possible and practical to do. If a business idea is feasible, research will show that there are enough people who will want to buy the service or product.

Feedback – Constructive and helpful comments that will help you to identify what you have done well and what you can improve.

Financial documents – Specific documents that are used to record the buying and selling of goods.

Flow chart – A list of tasks or stages that need to be completed, linked together in a specific order. Some tasks will need to be completed before others can be started. For example, you would need to type the letter in word-processing software before spell checking it.

Flow of mail – The process which mail goes through from when it is sent until it arrives at its destination.

Formal communication – Communication which uses professional language, and a record of what has been communicated is kept on record for future reference.

Formal meeting – A meeting between senior staff or a business and their suppliers or customers. Records are always kept.

Formal quote – This is when a business puts together a set of costs for a customer. For example, if you wanted to buy a computer, you might ask for a quote for a particular model. This would tell you how much you would pay if you decided to buy the computer.

Franking – The process of passing mail through a machine which franks a stamp on to it. The purpose of franking is to save time.

Functional areas – Different parts or departments of a business that focus on a limited range of important tasks.

Graphical communication – The use of visual images such as diagrams, illustrations or designs to convey meaning.

Health issue – A potential problem in the workplace that may affect a person's health.

Impression – The image of a person that someone is left with after talking to or dealing with another person.

Informal communication – Communication which uses 'everyday' language and is not kept on record for future reference.

Informal meetings – Often a meeting between colleagues. Records are rarely kept.

Instant Messaging (IM) – An instant text messaging service that happens in 'real time'.

Investment risk – a risk in business is often based on how likely it is that a business or investors will lose money.

Investors – People or businesses that give a business money. They invest in the business because they expect to receive some of the profits.

Invoice – A document sent to customers requesting payment for the supply of goods or services.

Leaked data – Information that is made available to the public when a business or individual wants to keep the information to themselves.

Legal duty – Something a business has got to do. If a business does not do their legal duty, they could be acting illegally.

Long term goals – Those which typically take between three and five years to complete. An example of a long-term goal could include an ambition to work in a management position within five years.

Manufacturing sector – This includes businesses that focus on making a product.

Medium term goals – Those which typically take between one and three years to complete. An example of a medium-term goal would be to gain work experience in a company that will allow you to get a full-time position or a higher level course of study.

Minutes – Minutes are a formal record of a meeting which highlight what has been agreed and who is taking responsibility for completing a particular task.

Motivation – Motivation is how much you want to do something. If you are highly motivated, it is likely that you enjoy your job and your work is of a high quality.

Multimedia Message Service (MMS) – Allows you to send and receive not only text but also sound, images and video.

Negative impression – When a customer receives poor service and bases their future opinions of the business on that view.

Open questions – Questions that require a longer answer – not just 'yes' or 'no'.

Pay – The amount of money received in return for working.

Policy – A principle or course of action adopted by an organisation or individual.

Poor posture – Positioning of the body which could cause long-term damage while working. Always try to adopt the correct posture.

Postal services – The term given to a range of different mail delivery companies.

Primary research – Original research carried out by you, for example a questionnaire.

Prioritise – Decide on the order for dealing with a number of tasks according to their relative importance.

Problem solving – The process of developing creative and flexible solutions to problems that may arise.

Procedure – A process for doing something, such as welcoming visitors or ordering stationery, that is set by the organisation.

Production costs – Any costs that are involved in the production of a product or the provision of a service.

Professional behaviour – Acting in a business-like manner. When receiving visitors, answering the telephone, etc., you are the public face of your employer. First impressions of an organisation are as important as first impressions of a person.

Professional demeanour – This is how someone appears in a first impression. If you are dressed smartly, are polite and helpful, and address the visitor's needs effectively, you are likely to be thought of as having a professional demeanour.

Profit – Money left over when all costs have been taken out of the turnover. In order to make the pie, Mulkern's Foods needs to spend a total of £1.50 on ingredients, making the pie and cooking the pie. The difference between what Mulkern's Foods spends to make the pie and the amount the customer pays for the pie is its profit.

Profit margin – The amount of profit expressed as a proportion of the turnover. So if a customer buys an item for £2, which costs £1.50 to produce, the profit margin is $33\frac{1}{3}$ per cent.

Promotion – When your employer rewards you by giving you a more important job. It often means earning more money.

Purpose of document – Each type of document performs a specific function. It is important that the correct document is used for the correct function if an administrative system is to work efficiently.

Recipient – Someone who receives something. In this case, someone who receives an email.

Responsibility – When you are responsible for a task, it is your duty to complete the task on time and follow any instructions you have been given.

Risk – A risk is the chance that something might happen. For example, if wires are trailing across a corridor there is a risk someone could trip over them.

Secondary research – Research carried out by another person which you have used in your work, for example a quotation from a book.

Self-management – The process of organising your time and your work in order to successfully complete tasks.

Selling costs – All the costs that are involved in selling a product.

Service sector – The service sector includes industries that provide a service such as banking and insurance.

Setting up a room – The process of making sure that rooms are set up and fit for the purpose of the meeting.

Short Message Service (SMS) – Allows you to send and receive text messages only up to 160 characters in length.

Short term goals – Those which typically take up to 12 months to achieve. An example of a short-term goal would be to achieve a qualification which will allow you to access a particular job or course of study.

Sorting – The process of putting mail into different piles so it can be distributed to the correct department.

Sources of information – Places where information can be found, to provide a realistic idea of the potential success of a business idea.

Stakeholder – Anybody with some form of interest in a business who stands to lose if it is run badly.

Targets – Things you want to achieve, also known as objectives. These are usually goals you want to complete in the next 6 or 12 months in order to improve your performance at work.

Tone – The way in which one person speaks to another person.

Transaction – The process of paying or receiving money for goods that have been bought or sold.

Turnover – Money coming into a business from customers. For example, if a customer buys a pie from Mulkern's shop for £2, this money counts towards the business's turnover.

Verbal communication – Talking to someone – or a group of people – to give them information.

Visitor's badge – A badge or security pass, identifying the visitor.

Work pattern – The way a person's working hours are organised, for example times, days of the week.

Index